STORING UP PROFITS

STORING UP PROFITS

Capitalize on
America's Obsession with STUFF
by Investing in Self-Storage

PAUL MOORE

BiggerPockets®
PUBLISHING
Denver, Colorado

Praise for

STORING UP PROFITS

"As the host of a real estate podcast with more than 2,000 episodes, I have interviewed quite a few syndicators and investors in the self-storage arena, but I have yet to see a helpful book on this topic. Paul Moore has written that book. Whether your goal is to build or buy and operate self-storage or just to invest, this book is a valuable guide to teach you the fundamentals at an understandable level."

**—Joe Fairless, author, podcast host,
and co-founder of Ashcroft Capital**

"The information [in this book] is the one-stop-shop to making self-storage part of your investing platform."

**—John Cohen, founder of Toro Real Estate Partners,
owner of JC Property Group, and co-host of
*The Real Estate Investing Experience***

"Paul understands that real estate is an amazing way to build wealth, keep up with inflation, and ethically lower your tax burden. [This book] is an amazing resource on how you can take advantage of these benefits and grow your wealth!"

**—Jake Stenziano, host of the podcast
*Wheelbarrow Profits***

"The world of self-storage investing can be a very lucrative one, but it is not as highlighted as many other real estate investment vehicles. Paul Moore's book is both timely and extremely well written ... [a] thorough explanation of what it takes to be successful with these types of investments. For any investor looking to diversify, it's a must-read."

—Matt Faircloth, co-founder of The DeRosa Group and author of *Raising Private Capital*

"I have been in the self-storage business for more than twenty-five years, and I have to say that this is one of the best and most complete books on the business of self-storage. ... A lot of good, useful information in between the covers of this one."

—Terry Campbell, executive vice president of Live Oak Bank's small business banking, America's top SBA self-storage lender

Storing Up Profits: Capitalize on America's Obsession with STUFF by Investing in Self-Storage
Paul Moore

Published by BiggerPockets Publishing LLC, Denver, Colorado
Copyright © 2021 by Paul Moore
All Rights Reserved.

Publisher's Cataloging-in-Publication Data
Names: Moore, Paul Thomas, 1963-, author.
Title: Storing up profits: capitalize on America's obsession with stuff by investing in self-storage / by Paul Moore.
Description: Includes bibliographical references. | Denver, CO: BiggerPockets Publishing, 2021.
Identifiers: LCCN: 2021939924 | ISBN: 9781947200487 (paperback) | 9781947200364 (ebook)
Subjects: LCSH Self-service storage facilities--United States. | Real estate investment--United States. | Personal finance. | BISAC BUSINESS & ECONOMICS / Real Estate / Commercial | BUSINESS & ECONOMICS / Real Estate / General | BUSINESS & ECONOMICS / Investments & Securities / Real Estate | BUSINESS & ECONOMICS / Personal Finance / Investing
Classification: LCC HD255 .M66 2021 | DDC 332.63/24--dc23

Published in the United States of America
Printed in the USA on recycled paper
10 9 8 7 6 5 4 3 2 1

Dedication

I want to thank my wife, Elaine. I can't believe you agreed to join this entrepreneurial journey thirty-four years ago, and I'm so glad you did! I also want to thank our awesome children, Jonathon, Hannah, Mary, and Abby. You have put up with a lot, and I'm very grateful for your patience.

TABLE OF CONTENTS

INTRODUCTION

I am a recovering shiny object chaser. Six years before beginning my journey in self-storage, I had worked with a partner to build, operate, and sell a very successful quasi-multifamily/quasi-hotel in North Dakota. Then I helped him develop a beautiful Hyatt House hotel that ultimately bit the dust.

Before those ventures, I had been a serial real estate entrepreneur, flipping dozens of houses and pricey waterfront lots, buying two small subdivisions, creating a waterfront real estate website, building nine homes, appearing on HGTV, and much more. I'd done rent-to-owns, owner financing, lease-option sandwiches, notes, you name it.

I made a lot of money along the way. But I also lost a good bit of money—and time. My dear wife was tired of all the restarts and ramp-ups and promises. And I was exhausted. I was in my fifties, and after watching my friend's Hyatt crash and burn, I decided I didn't want to be on the wrong side of a downturn if there should come a day that I could no longer work. We have four great kids, and all were still pre-college.

I had some cash in the bank from the North Dakota deal, and I decided to galvanize my focus. I would choose one path that made the most sense, and I would commit to that path for the rest of my life. That path was commercial real estate investing. More specifically, I landed on value-add commercial multifamily investing.

As I surveyed the wreckage of some of my past speculative escapades, I determined that more than anything else, I needed to learn the difference between *speculating* and *investing*.

Investing Versus Speculating

Investing is when your principal is generally safe with a chance to make a return. Speculating is when your principal is *not at all* safe with a chance to make a return.

It's fine to do either, as long as you are conscious of the choice you are making and able to live with the outcome. Some of the world's most legendary investment stories come to us from speculators—like the Stanford professor who gave Google $100,000 and parlayed it into more than a billion dollars. Or the guy in your town and mine who bought a condemned property on the courthouse steps and got it rezoned for ten times the profit.

Such stories become the stuff of legend because they are the exceptions. The vast majority of wealth is made and preserved by investors with simple, low-risk, buy-and-hold strategies, like those of Warren Buffett. He has said he would rather invest in chewing gum than internet stocks because he couldn't predict how technology would change over the coming decades. However, he observed that "the internet will never change the way people chew gum."

I reflected on some of my investing, which had actually been speculating.

- The $75,000 dropped into an oil well that never produced a drop.
- The $90,000 and years of effort invested in a wireless internet startup that got its wires crossed in the frozen North Dakota winter.
- The $100,000 invested with a foreign exchange trader located in Charlotte, Virginia who had a "proprietary methodology" for returning 2 to 3 percent per month. That was in 1999, and he is now in year 18 or so of his 157-year federal prison sentence. He still won't tell the FBI and 2,000 other investors which offshore accounts he hid our $18 million in.
- The time I got a high loan-to-value (LTV) ratio loan to buy an overpriced five-acre waterfront lot with hopes that the gravel road would soon be public and allow me to sell my subdivided five one-acre lots for a 100 percent profit. (This one actually worked out, and I made a huge profit. Sometimes speculation pays off!)

I was done with shaky speculation and ready to focus solely on safe commercial real estate—multifamily real estate specifically. The team at my company, Wellings Capital, was committed to never knowingly overpaying for any apartment acquisition.

The problem was timing: we were late to the party. Multifamily had become the darling of the real estate world, and it seemed as if everyone had been running after it since the middle of the recession. I had learned multifamily from the ground up in our North Dakota development and operation, but my team and I wanted to learn even more about value-add multifamily investing. To do so, we joined an expensive yearlong mentoring program. We read books, evaluated deals, walked properties, performed due diligence, and analyzed financials. We formed an investment firm and built a website—and then another one. We renamed the company, designed brochures, and started blogging and podcasting. I got involved on BiggerPockets.com. Over time, we began acquiring a pool of investors and started analyzing deals and making offers, although we were continually outbid. As we watched the market climb and then climb some more, we waited for the right multifamily deal at a fair price—or for the market to turn down.

Finally, all the pieces fell into place when our new firm acquired multifamily properties in partnership with an experienced asset manager. We took the investment process seriously, and investors liked the way we approached the deal and the details of the process. They soon began to ask about the next opportunity.

I had to tell these repeat and prospective investors that I didn't know. In reviewing our history, accounting for our extreme conservative bias, and surveying the continuing craze for multifamily investing, I suspected it would likely not be soon—possibly even years.

This was no way to build a company. And since a commercial real estate syndicator's income is largely weighted on the back end—giving investors the lion's share of the profits for the first several years—this was no way to build a sustainable income either. (I had already blown through most of the funds I pocketed from the successful sale of our North Dakota property.)

That's when I got the call from Kris.

He started by telling me about his history with investing and operating ground-up and value-add multifamily projects. Then he went on to ask, "Would you like to hear why I love self-storage?"

Good thing this wasn't a video call. Kris might have seen me roll my eyes or noticed I was only feigning interest.

The call was not expected or even particularly welcome, but his multifamily track record was impressive and his enthusiasm for self-storage was evident—and a bit infectious. I decided to hear him out, even though I was reluctant. In just 30 minutes, Kris had opened my eyes to the enormous opportunities available in self-storage. He convinced me that the parallels to multifamily were real, meaning my experience was relevant to this new investment. He also showed me that, contrary to my preconceived opinion, the opportunities for value-adds in self-storage often exceed those in multifamily. Lastly, he made me aware that self-storage performed similarly to (actually better than) multifamily in the recession and beyond, which was an important investment thesis for our firm.

This brief call led to a two-and-a-half-hour Saturday call, which led to a trip to the headquarters of Kris's favorite self-storage syndicator. Then another. Then multiple trips to the field to see assets in person.

A new era was born. Well, sort of—I still needed to convince my wife that I wasn't chasing another shiny object. (I wish you could have been there during that conversation.) It sounded all too familiar, and she was skeptical. After all, sheet metal and concrete aren't the sexiest things on the planet. But a growing bank account *is* pretty sexy, and the guy who makes it grow is her hero once again.

Since that phone call, my firm, Wellings Capital, has invested over $53 million in recession-resistant commercial real estate assets with a variety of operators. We've focused on self-storage, investing in 142 self-storage facilities within the U.S. with a total of over 520,000 units and over 8 million square feet. Our self-storage portfolio offers diversification across different asset classes, geographies, operating partners, strategies, and properties.

That's the beginning of my story, and I'm sticking with it. And I'm sticking with self-storage investing. If you want to find opportunities not seen in any other asset class, increase your income, and grow your wealth exponentially, read on.

Why I Love Self-Storage

The main message of this book is to take advantage of America's obsession with stuff—and there's a reason for that. The self-storage industry is *booming.* The total number of U.S. storage facilities is about the same as the number of Starbucks, McDonald's, and Subways *combined.* Self-storage can also be profitable in almost any market because people will always have excess stuff. This industry is also recession resistant, and it strengthens in economic booms. You'll have the opportunity to respond in real time to changing market conditions through short leases and dynamic revenue management. The self-storage industry also performs well in times of crises, since new tenants are derived from the four Ds: divorce, downsizing, dislocation, and death.

On a less morbid note, you won't have to deal with the same frustrations you normally would with traditional real estate investments. First things first: no toilets. Say goodbye to plumbing nightmares. Also, there will be no underground water main breaks. (Wellings Capital once repaired a water main at one of our apartments. Current tally: $107,000.) As a matter of fact, life will be easier when you don't have tenants living in your investment: no arguments about security deposits, no middle of the night phone calls, no more complicated evictions (since it's easier to evict stuff than people). Tenants will also be more sticky (since they're typically not price-sensitive), and storage tends to be a small part of most tenants' budgets.

Like I said earlier, self-storage isn't sexy—but the profits are. With auto-billing on credit cards with monthly contracts, it's easier to raise rents. Also, rent is collateralized by belongings, making it inconvenient for tenants to move. You'll love the excellent cash flow self-storage produces as well as the multitude of ancillary income opportunities. When it comes to adding value to your facility, you can do so at low cost—like reconfiguring units to meet current demand. Your operating and maintenance costs will be low and predictable, unlike the many unpredictable factors in multifamily investing. And you won't have stiff competition in that many mom-and-pop owners are behind the curve on technology for management and marketing. (These facilities can also be easy acquisition targets.)

The benefits to self-storage investing are nearly endless. As you dive deeper into this book, you'll see all the opportunities available to you to make a profit!

Book Breakdown

This book is broken down into three sections: the basics, strategies to be successful, and lastly, mastering self-storage investing.

Section I is designed to give you an overview of the powerful drivers that make self-storage such a great investment. I'll review the powerful supply-and-demand characteristics of this industry and the importance of fragmentation among self-storage owners. I'll expand on why I love this industry, and you'll read about how revenue, profit, and value are generated. Then, I'll explore the four pillars of profit and the many tax benefits of investing in self-storage. Finally, I'll discuss the mindset of the world's most successful investors.

Section II moves beyond *the Big Why* and encourages you to think about *the Big How*. As in any business, there are a variety of strategies to successfully build your brand and compound your wealth, which won't all be covered in this book. However, my goal is to give you an overview of the major routes taken by syndicators to grow a self-storage operation. Though you may be planning a passive investment, it will be important for you to be aware of these strategies so you can decide what level of risk you are most comfortable with and what return profile you can expect. Knowing these strategies will arm you with the right questions to ask your syndicator as well. I'm going to discuss three major strategies for self-storage success, which will be split up into three chapters:
1. Ground-Up Development
2. Value-Add Self-Storage
3. Retrofit and Repurpose an Existing Building

Section III explores the numerous reasons why it is hard to get into large-scale commercial real estate investing. Anything *this* good can't be accessed casually. If you hear otherwise, I'd recommend you run in most cases (minus one exception). This section is designed to jump-start your thinking and provide you with a variety of potential paths to start your self-storage career. The seven paths I cover will help the vast majority of readers not only gain access to the exclusive club of self-storage investing but also master it.

SECTION I
WHY SELF-STORAGE?

CHAPTER 1

THE BASICS OF SELF-STORAGE

When I originally heard about self-storage, it sounded awfully boring. Where are the value-adds? We're talking about four pieces of sheet metal, some rivets, a door, and a slab of concrete. No countertops to upgrade. No cabinets. No carpet or hardwoods. Multifamily just seemed a lot more exciting. Perhaps that's why multifamily podcasts and books and training programs abound, while those for self-storage are rare.

I was surprised to learn that self-storage has a wide variety of value-add opportunities. As I will demonstrate later, there may be more value-add opportunities in self-storage than in most multifamily properties currently. This trend may continue for years to come due to the fractional nature of self-storage ownership in the United States versus higher corporate ownership in the more mature and consolidated multifamily realm.

Check out the same-property net operating income (NOI) growth in these various commercial asset classes. Manufactured housing and self-storage lead the pack!

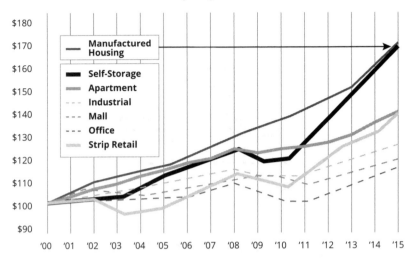

Same-Property NOI Growth

Source: SNI Financial "Indexed Same Store NOI Growth Publicly Traded REITs." Assumes $100 starting point

Self-storage has intrinsically powerful drivers behind its income and equity growth. We'll review many of these in the coming chapters, but one of the reasons for this sector's recent surge in popularity among investors is *overflow*. There is overflow from other asset classes, such as single-family and multifamily. As of now, multifamily is overheated and pricing has reached such a boiling point that investors of all sizes are looking for value elsewhere.

This can be good news for self-storage syndicators and investors, but it can also mean that this sector is becoming overcrowded too. As we'll see, the fragmented nature of self-storage ownership plays a balancing role here.

Why Is Self-Storage Hot?

Self-storage shares several characteristics with multifamily. For instance, multifamily economics are based on commercial real estate valuation principles. Later, you'll see that this is a powerful driver toward your investing success and perhaps the reason that most of the world's wealthiest invest in commercial real estate. (Hopefully you're about to join them.)

Like self-storage, multifamily has powerful demographic drivers that are predictable for decades to come. Baby boomers, millennials, immigrants, and Gen Z tenants are all flocking to multifamily. Additionally, both self-storage and multifamily performed well during the last downturn, with very few foreclosures. Government faux pas, complicit lenders, and irresponsible buyers starting in the mid-1990s drove an unnatural homeownership boom that burst in the mid-to-late 2000s. Multifamily has been on the rise ever since.

Unlike self-storage, though, multifamily is a sexy asset class. Apartments are a cool investment; self-storage is decidedly uncool. That made it difficult to get excited at first. But I soon learned that the value-add opportunities in self-storage actually outweigh those of multifamily. While many of the demographic drivers are the same, the tenants are far stickier (less likely to leave due to rent increases), and the market is far more fragmented. (Fragmented markets, those dominated by mom-and-pop operators, provide some of the best opportunities in the real estate world.) Plus, self-storage is easier and less costly to manage. All these qualities make self-storage much more exciting than multifamily at this moment, and frankly, I believe it's a better opportunity.

Self-storage, like multifamily, can be overheated. But this is true only in certain locations rather than throughout the entire market. The fragmented nature of this asset class creates opportunities that simply don't exist in the multifamily and single-family space right now. I'll explore these in detail later.

Self-Storage by the Numbers

1. According to the Self Storage Association (SSA), the self-storage industry has been one of the fastest-growing sectors of the U.S. commercial real estate industry for more than 40 years.[1]
2. Total rentable U.S. self-storage space is approximated to be over 2.3 billion square feet. This represents more than 78 square miles of rentable self-storage space—three times the size of Manhattan—and a total storage capacity of 7.3 square feet for every person in the United States.[2]

---

1 https://www.selfstorage.org/LinkClick.aspx?fileticket=fJYAow6_AU0%3D&portalid=0

2 https://www.laingselfstorage.com/post/2017/05/15/5-facts-about-storage

3. The SSA breaks down the distribution of self-storage facilities as 36 percent urban, 51 percent suburban, and 12 percent rural.[3]
4. Approximate national average monthly rental rates are $1.25 per square foot (non-climate-controlled) and $1.60 per square foot (climate-controlled) for a 10 × 10 unit.[4]
5. The national average occupancy rate for self-storage facilities is 92 percent as of 2018, according to Neighbor.com.[5]
6. The 2020 Self Storage Demand Study estimates that 10.6 percent of U.S. households rent a self-storage unit.[6]
7. The SSA puts the average size of a "primary" U.S. self-storage facility (a storage facility that is the main source of revenue for a business) at about 57,000 square feet, and the average facility size is 546 units.[7]
8. Facilities offering boat and/or RV storage total 18.7 percent; 31 percent offer truck rentals.[8]
9. The top six companies (U-Haul and five real estate investment trusts) own about 12 percent of all self-storage facilities, according to the SSA.[9] That amounts to about 31 percent of all rentable self-storage square footage.[10]
10. Neighbor.com estimates that about 17 percent of all self-storage renters will rent for less than three months; 20 percent for three to six months; 17 percent for seven to twelve months; 21 percent for one to two years; and 15 percent for three to five years. The average rental duration is 14 months.[11]
11. Approximately 72 percent of self-storage tenants live in a single-family home and 26 percent live in an apartment or condo, according to the SSA.[12]

---

3 Self Storage Association, *Self Storage Demand Study 2020 Edition* (Self Storage Association: Alexandria, VA, 2020), p 6.

4 https://www.selfstorage.org/LinkClick.aspx?fileticket=fJYAow6_AU0%3D&portalid=0

5 https://www.neighbor.com/storage-blog/self-storage-industry-statistics/

6 SSA, *Self Storage 2020*, p 4.

7 https://www.selfstorage.org/LinkClick.aspx?fileticket=fJYAow6_AU0=&portalid=0

8 Ibid.

9 Ibid.

10 https://www.sparefoot.com/self-storage/news/1432-self-storage-industry-statistics/

11 https://www.neighbor.com/storage-blog/self-storage-industry-statistics/

12 SSA, *Self Storage 2020*, p 18.

12. Approximately 68 percent of tenants have a garage but still rent a unit, 53 percent have an attic in their home, and 40 percent have a basement.[13]
13. The income of 61 percent of self-storage tenants is less than $75,000 annually; 44 percent have an income of under $50,000.[14]
14. Of self-storage tenants, around 4 percent are military personnel.[15]
15. About 84 percent of all U.S. counties have at least one "primary" self-storage facility.[16]

Self-Storage: A Brief History

According to Neighbor.com, ancient China is the birthplace of self-storage, though there is no hard evidence to back up this claim. Other stories tell of enterprising British explorers who stored personal contents at a bank while they sailed away. When the banks filled up, their items were brought to a warehouse.[17] This is all speculation, so take this with a grain of salt. But it's not hard to believe that for as long as humans have been on the move, they've needed places to hold their stuff.

When it comes to the history of self-storage in America, the facts are clearer. Brothers Martin and John Bekins of Omaha, Nebraska, founded the Bekins Van and Storage Co. in the 1890s. The business entailed three horse-drawn vans, aka buggies. They later expanded to Los Angeles, California, and eventually built the city's first reinforced steel and concrete warehouse building. They expanded across southern California in the first half of the 20th century.

According to SpareFoot.com, the first facility with garage doors was constructed in 1964 by Russ Williams and Bob Munn in Odessa, Texas, for the oil industry. I'm not sure about their marketing acumen, since they succinctly named their facility A-1 U-Store-It U-Lock-It U-Carry-The-Key. The facility was created for oil workers to store their tools and supplies. Other companies followed their model, and an industry was born.[18]

---

13 SSA, *Self Storage 2020*, p 18.

14 Ibid.

15 Ibid.

16 https://www.selfstorage.org/LinkClick.aspx?fileticket=fJYAow6_AU0=&portalid=0

17 https://www.neighbor.com/storage-blog/history-of-self-storage/

18 "A Brief History of Self-Storage," SpareFoot, last modified January 18, 2013, https://www.sparefoot.com/self-storage/blog/3230-a-brief-history-of-self-storage/.

It's interesting to speculate about the change in mindset of Americans from the Great Depression to the recent Great Recession and how self-storage played into that change. I've seen photos of furniture—chests of drawers, couches, bed frames—left along the road during the Depression, perhaps abandoned by people making the brutal trip west to California in search of work on farms.

I don't recall seeing any photos like that from the recent recession. Do you? These days, I can't imagine most Americans ditching their stuff, especially with the opportunity to utilize self-storage at a relatively low cost (compared to a mortgage or the rent for an apartment). Perhaps that's one of the reasons self-storage weathered the last recession relatively well compared to other asset classes.

Who's Renting Self-Storage?

As you can see in the following graphic, almost 50 percent of the customers in this 2020 study are long-term residential tenants. The second-largest group is short-term residential tenants, followed by commercial operators, and a few other segments.

Major Market Segmentation

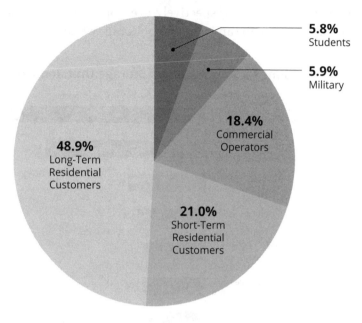

5.8%
Students

5.9%
Military

18.4%
Commercial
Operators

48.9%
Long-Term
Residential
Customers

21.0%
Short-Term
Residential
Customers

Source: www.ibisworld.com

Why Are People Renting Self-Storage?

Industry experts often reference life's four Ds as the reasons for self-storage demand. These are:

- Downsizing
- Divorce
- Death
- Dislocation

The first three are self-evident. The last D refers to a variety of situations, such as a renter relocating and needing temporary space or a couple moving in together and facing a temporary situation of duplicate furnishings.

A Self Storage Association (SSA) self-storage demand study breaks down a dozen reasons people use self-storage. The top two by far, at 42 percent and 33 percent respectively, are storage of items that users don't have space for at home and temporary storage while changing residences.

Reasons for Renting a Self-Storage Unit: Individuals

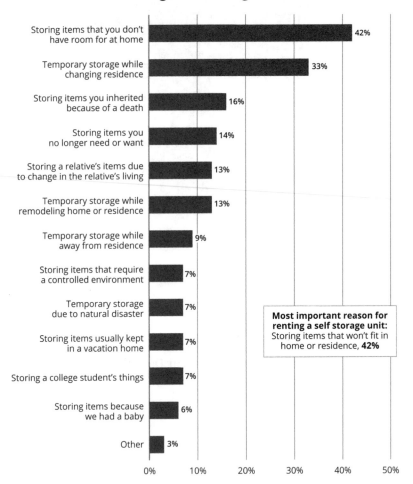

Source: SS Demand Study 2020. Note: Respondents could select more than one option.

Like individual consumers, businesses have a variety of reasons for renting self-storage as well. Here is a breakdown from the 2020 demand study.

Reasons for Renting a Self-Storage Unit: Businesses

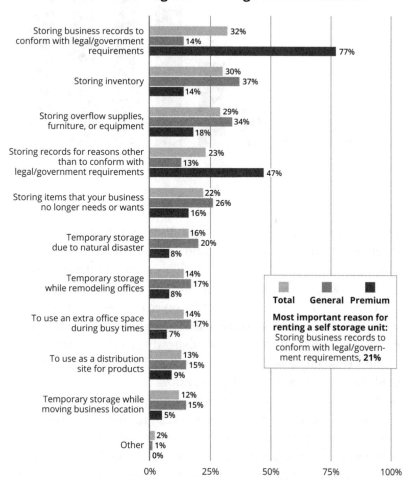

Source: SS Demand Study 2020. Note: Respondents could select more than one option.

What has been the impact of the sector's popularity on self-storage construction over the past decade and a half? Self-storage construction spending has risen from under $500 million in 2013 to around $4.5 billion in 2020, as you can see in the following chart .

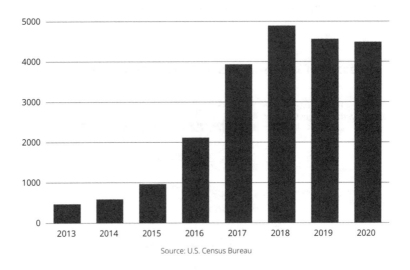

Self-Storage Construction Spending by Month 2013–present

Source: U.S. Census Bureau

Perhaps you're concerned that the self-storage business is overbuilt and you may be too late. That is a valid concern and should not be taken lightly. In the next chapter we will consider the powerful role of fragmentation in providing continuing opportunities in the self-storage sector.

What's the bottom line for you? If you're interested in self-storage, these statistics should give you cause for cautious optimism. Did I hear you say, "Wait, that's it? You're just advocating *cautious optimism*?"

Before this phrase scares you away, consider that this is where you should always be as a prospective investor.

- It was *wild optimism* that drove the tulip bulb craze (aka tulip mania) of 1636. It ended in an awful crash in 1637, and many lost fortunes. Lest you think those investors were cavemen...
- It was *wild optimism* that drove investors to make unsound bets on overpriced tech stocks in the late 1990s, only to watch their fortunes dry up a few years later.
- It was *wild optimism* that drove Bitcoin to dizzying heights in 2021, before it lost about half of its value in a few days.

That's why I'm not a huge fan of wild optimism, at least when it takes the form of irrational exuberance. Even though wild optimism may not be my favorite, there are stories of wild profits that have been made, and are consistently being made, in this sector. I've included several of them in this volume, but let's start with Todd Allen's story.

More Than 37 Percent Annual ROI from a Value-Add Self-Storage Deal

Todd Allen is an experienced self-storage operator and syndicator. His Georgia-based firm, Reliant Real Estate Management, has grown into one of the nation's foremost self-storage operators. My company, Wellings Capital, invests with Todd in both of its diversified real estate investment funds.

Reliant acquired a mom-and-pop self-storage facility in Gainesville, Georgia, in January 2017. The facility consisted of 53,000 net rentable square feet (NRSF) with 419 units. There was a mix of standard drive-up units and climate-controlled storage units. The gross rental revenue was $45,000 per month at the time of acquisition.

As at many mom-and-pop facilities, the rents were about 15 to 20 percent below market. Their "other income" from ancillary sales (locks, boxes, tape, scissors, etc.) was virtually zero.

All of the competitors were mom-and-pop operators with hardly any ancillary sales, truck rentals, or professional marketing strategies. Despite this, these operators had strong occupancy and higher-than-average rental rates. A market study showed an undersupply of 85,000 square feet of storage in a five-mile radius. (You will learn how to calculate this later.)

The site itself had natural characteristics that made it ideal for a value-add/redevelopment project, including two acres of undeveloped land in front of the existing facility. It was also visibly located on the main road in Gainesville's revitalized commercial district. With traffic counts of 18,000 vehicles per day, this was a wonderful situation for Todd and the Reliant team. Their business plan focused on repositioning the facility to a Class A, institutional-grade self-storage facility.

After acquisition, Reliant went to work constructing a two-story, 30,000-gross-square-foot climate-controlled building in front of the existing facilities. This building included an office and showroom as well as an apartment for the new on-site manager.

I visited this facility about the time construction was completed. The new building added 20,000 climate-controlled NRSF to the operation, which added $32,000 to the facility's potential monthly revenue. When the new building opened, physical occupancy dropped from around 90 percent to 60 percent (due to the increased number of units). However, due to the facility's increased visibility on the main road, enhanced unit mix, improved marketing, and well-trained manager, the facility was able lease up at about 4 percent per month and returned to 92 percent stabilized occupancy in only eight months.

The total all-in cost to acquire and improve this facility was $7.4 million. This consisted of $3.9 million in debt (53 percent LTV) and $3.5 million in equity (cash from investors). The facility currently provides a net cash flow of $300,000 annually to investors (8.5 percent annual cash-on-cash return).

The site is well-positioned to sell to an institutional buyer, such as a real estate investment trust (REIT). Institutional buyers have been acquiring assets like this in the 4.5 to 5.5 percent cap rate (expected rate of return) range from Reliant and similar operators. If the facility was sold today (two and a half years into the project) for a 5 percent cap rate, the price would be $11 million. Reliant feels that continuing to push rents and other income for the next year will actually get them to a $12 million exit price.

Let's do some quick math. If Todd sells the property for $11 million, assuming no principal paydown on the debt, his investors will take home about $7 million ($11 million minus $3.9 million debt minus closing costs). They invested only $3.5 million in cash, so this is 100 percent appreciation on their invested capital in 30 months. If you assume only 18 months' cash flow as well, that is an additional $450,000. The total return is therefore about 113 percent.

If achieved in three years, that is an annual return on investment (ROI) of over 37 percent. And it's likely that the investors paid zero in income taxes along the way. They could even delay capital gains taxes if Reliant sells the property with a 1031 tax-deferred exchange.

Is this type of deal normal? Certainly not in most businesses, but it is fairly normal for Todd and his company, which has documented deals like this at least 21 times in the past several years. Is it possible to replicate? It most certainly is, and I have seen it done time and time again.

The point is to get you excited about self-storage and to give you an idea about what is possible. The fragmented (mom-and-pop) nature of ownership in the self-storage arena and the opportunity to add value, add capacity, or repurpose empty buildings are providing a unique window of opportunity. You'll be able to build projects that will benefit the community, profit investors, and build your wealth. You may even have a lot of fun along the way.

CHAPTER 2
THE POWER OF SELF-STORAGE

There are over 49,000 self-storage facilities in the United States, and the great news is that a large percentage of them are run by independent operators.[19] Many of these are mom-and-pop shops, and they run their facilities that way. They believe they don't need to run them better: they're making a profit, and they're happy. And compressed cap rates mean that their facilities (even the mediocre ones) are worth far more than they ever dreamed.

The following graphic shows the approximate breakdown of ownership of self-storage facilities in the United States. Note that the 72 percent of facilities that are owned by independent operators are not necessarily poorly run. But typically, even if they are well managed, there is room for improvement, which can be implemented by a great operator.

---

[19] MiniCo, *2021 Self-Storage Almanac*

Self-Storage Ownership

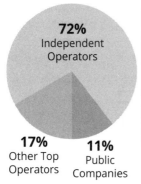

72% Independent Operators

17% Other Top Operators

11% Public Companies

Source: 2020 Self-Storage Almanac

Contrast ownership of self-storage with multifamily right now. The apartment world has been increasingly dominated by larger, well-capitalized players, and it is hard to acquire an underperforming property.

Single vs. Multiple Apartment Owners

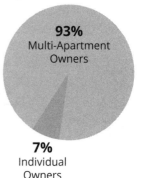

93% Multi-Apartment Owners

7% Individual Owners

Source: National Multifamily Housing Council Website

12 Common Characteristics of Mom-and-Pop Storage Shops

1. **If you build it, they will come**: This worked in the early days of the business, and some operators still cling to this approach.

2. **No website or a poor one**: The business was largely characterized by drive-by marketing for years, and this still works for many. (But can they really maximize revenue? They often don't need to.)

3. **No showroom**: The opportunity for ancillary income is not a priority.

4. **Rare price increases**: Many small operators become friendly with their tenants and rarely raise rents. The result is below-market pricing.

5. **Across-the-board pricing**: While a savvy operator might raise the price on their last few units of a popular size, this is often too much trouble for a small operator.

6. **Rent what we have**: Storage facilities are mostly sheet metal and rivets. Units can usually be reconfigured to meet current demand. For example, if the demand for 10 × 10s is high and 10 × 20s are empty, walls and doors can be added to optimize occupancy and income. Most small operators wouldn't bother with this.

7. **Poor maintenance**: Some of the 1970s and 1980s facilities look like, well, facilities from the 1970s and 1980s. There is little reason to update them or maintain them well, and revenues reflect this.

8. **Poor security**: The No. 1 crime at self-storage facilities is theft (obviously), and many smaller operators don't go to the trouble of installing camera security and gated fencing.

9. **No marketing budget**: Many of these operators boast that their marketing budget is close to zero (except for that donation to get their name in the charity raffle brochure). Their revenues suffer, but they may not know or care.

10. **Untapped land**: Many operators have unused land or parking lots for RVs and boats that could be used for profitable expansion through a beautiful, new climate-controlled building.

11. **Pest control and water infiltration**: Many facilities get a bad reputation. In 1999, when my antique furniture was roach-infested and water-stained, I wasn't a happy self-storage customer.

12. **Rental truck income**: Rental truck operations (such as U-Haul and Penske) can often be a great source of ancillary income with little capital expense or effort. In addition to a healthy boost to the bottom line and asset value, they can also lift occupancy by 3 to 5 percent. Most small operators don't go to the trouble.

The Power of Acquiring from a Mom-and-Pop

This fragmentation means that there are many acquisition opportunities unique to the self-storage asset class. A lot of facilities won't be candidates, but the sheer number of facilities means that there are plenty of targets to go around.

Would-be buyers should target mom-and-pop facilities that are:

- In the path of progress.
- On a highly traveled road (traffic count of 10,000-plus vehicles per day), with great visibility along that road.
- In an area where neighboring land is unavailable or cost-prohibitive.
- Large enough to achieve economies of scale or possible to expand.
- In an underserved location. (The national average self-storage density is about seven square feet per person in a three- to five-mile radius, though it varies by region and local demographics. This analysis can be quickly estimated at the RadiusPlus website and elsewhere.)

Acquiring an underperforming independently operated facility has so many advantages for an operator/investor. It involves less risk and hassle than ground-up construction, and it can provide significant upsides when it comes to income and value. I will demonstrate later that the economic benefits of taking a mom-and-pop facility to a professionally run operation are almost unparalleled.

The Power of Operating Like a Franchise

Small operators often view their facilities as a passive parcel of real estate that throws off mailbox money. That's fine for them, and it works for most. But if you have the desire to take an asset like that and apply best-in-class marketing and operations practices, you may be able to create income for yourself and your investors and add millions to your net worth. Great investors apply a variety of professional operations and marketing techniques to turn a lagging facility into a best-in-market operation.

QUICK INSIGHTS

The Law of Inertia

Please keep this in mind: Self-storage does not have the same marketing draw that some other businesses enjoy. For example, people can often be convinced that they are missing out if they don't have the latest tech toys or gadgets. But you can't create demand where it doesn't exist: if a person doesn't have stuff to store, you can't convince them to rent a storage unit.

You also usually can't convince someone who is storing their stuff with a competitor to move it to your nicer, newer facility. "Sticky tenants" are one of the most powerful drivers of success in this business. Once you have tenants, you'll probably keep them if you treat them well. The law of inertia works powerfully in self-storage: An object at rest tends to stay at rest.

I once visited a midsize operator our fund invests with and toured their new headquarters, which was equipped with a first-rate classroom where new managers go through a weeklong training program to learn how to market and run a facility. I was surprised at how many strategies and techniques are available to optimize operations and improve marketing. Here are just a few:

- Partner with local moving companies. (They have advanced intel about when people are moving in and out.)
- Advertise to local e-commerce businesses. (They often need a place to store inventory.)
- Become a preferred vendor at the local real estate association.
- Add a billboard to your property.
- Sign a cell tower lease on your property. (This can add $1,000 or more to your monthly income.)
- Add a liquid propane sale kiosk.
- Add an ATM.
- Charge late fees and administration fees.
- Debit client bank accounts using ACH, debit cards, or recurrently charge on a credit card.
- Raise rates in the heat of summer and in the middle of the busy holiday season.
- Stage your showroom with colors and a smart traffic path to appeal to potential customers' emotions and to safety-minded prospects.
- Offer a free truck rental to those moving in. (They can pay for their own when they leave.)

I know a savvy midsize operator who uses Facebook, casual conversations with tenants, LexisNexis, and other smart data-gathering techniques. Why? By understanding his individual tenant's income level, motivation, job title, past location, storage contents, and more, he can determine how much of a rent increase each tenant might tolerate. A tenant who has just moved from New York City for an executive promotion and will be building a new home for the next 14 months is unlikely to move due to two modest rent bumps. But a price shopper who's just storing "junk" long term could pack up and leave anytime.

Self-storage also provides the opportunity to immediately respond to changing market conditions. If you operate commercial office, retail, or manufacturing properties, you're locked into a few tenants with long-term leases. Self-storage operators can change their rates and advertising within minutes and see the impact within hours. The opportunity to use dynamic revenue management provides flexibility to a smart owner and a well-run facility. This is somewhat unique to self-storage, and mom-and-pop owners rarely take advantage of this inherent benefit.

The following graphics show how self-storage tenants learn of and make first contact with a facility. Of potential renters, 43 percent choose to visit a storage facility in person the first time, and 23 percent of renters first learned about their chosen facility by driving past it. This would support my point about the benefit of having a visible location on a main road. The world is also obviously going to continue in the digital direction, so as those trends progress, facilities with updated and user-friendly websites and a strong digital platform will get a disproportionate share of future business. Public Storage, the largest player in this space, spends a boatload for online marketing; and it's reported that they get a much higher percentage of their business from this avenue.

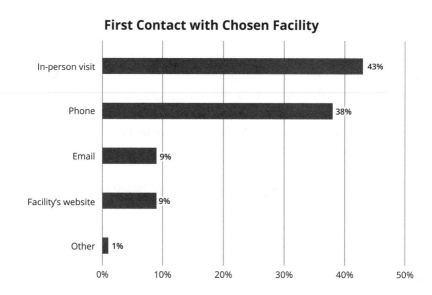

First Contact with Chosen Facility

Source: SS Demand Study 2020

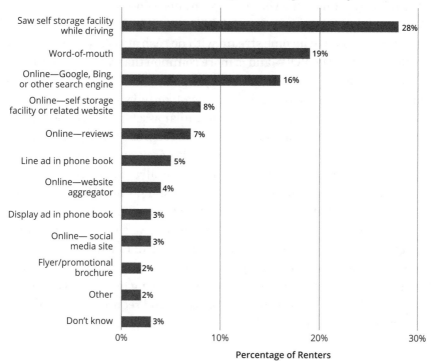

Means of First Learning of Storage Facility

Means	Percentage
Saw self storage facility while driving	28%
Word-of-mouth	19%
Online—Google, Bing, or other search engine	16%
Online—self storage facility or related website	8%
Online—reviews	7%
Line ad in phone book	5%
Online—website aggregator	4%
Display ad in phone book	3%
Online— social media site	3%
Flyer/promotional brochure	2%
Other	2%
Don't know	3%

Percentage of Renters

Source: SS Demand Study 2020

If you think this is a simple business, you've got it wrong. It's simple to run a basic self-storage operation as a passive asset. It's complex to run self-storage as a full-time, revenue- and value-maximizing business. This is not a passive income generation play. That is, unless you find a great operator who is doing all this stuff right and you passively invest with them. Then you may be able to achieve the best of both worlds.

As we will see later, if you can buy a mom-and-pop asset the right way and bring it up to professional standards, you may be able to create significant income for yourself and your investors. In addition to the ongoing income, you should be able to achieve significant value by refinancing the debt or selling to a larger player, such as a REIT.

Refinancing or Selling to an Institutional Buyer

If you can convert your small-time asset to a best-in-class operation, you will be able to achieve much higher income levels and potentially unlock a lot of value by refinancing your debt. Many operators are able to refinance all of their (and their investors') original principal back out of the deal, leaving them a profitable income stream with no cash at risk. This effectively results in an infinite ROI—and is more common than you would think.

You may also be positioned to be acquired by a REIT or another institutional buyer. If your operation is franchise-like and your revenue is stabilized, and especially if you have several similar assets in a portfolio, a REIT may come knocking at your door. REITs are often cash-heavy and looking for stabilized, predictable income with little hassle and drama. They seek well-located assets where the heavy lifting has already been done.

This can be a bonus for you and your investors, since REITs will often pay extra to get what they want. Their operators and investors are willing to pay a premium to minimize drama and achieve a predictable income stream. They also want to write larger checks. REITs will typically pay a premium for a portfolio of homogenous assets because uniform operations lead to economies of scale and higher net operating income (NOI). Plus, a portfolio sale reduces the transactional costs and requires less time than constructing a similar portfolio through individual acquisitions.

Portfolio Premium

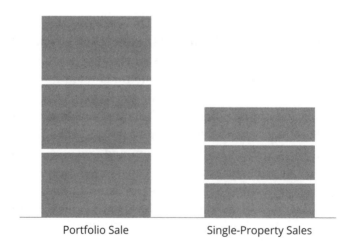

Portfolio Sale   Single-Property Sales

We'll talk about this much more later, but here is a quick preview of the power of buying right and selling to a REIT. A REIT bought several facilities that my friend (who our fund invests with) operated. Though the going rate for these types of facilities was about a 7 percent cap rate, the REIT paid about 5.5 percent (lower percent = higher price). This one maneuver—selling to a REIT—created about a 27 percent increase in value at the asset level.

But it was much better than that. Because the seller had 60 percent leverage on his assets, he was able to multiply the asset-level appreciation by 2.5 (1 / (100% − 60%) = 2.5). The operator and his equity investors actually benefited by equity appreciation of over 67 percent (27% × 2.5).

That didn't even include all the other income and value that was generated by the operator's/seller's implementation of professional operations and marketing, which generated far more.

Sticky Tenant Base

Self-storage has among the stickiest tenant bases of any real estate asset class. Imagine this scenario: You're renting an apartment. You like it there, but it's the same old thing month in and month out, and you plan to rent for years to come. You get a notice that your rent is going up by 6 percent. You're paying $1,000 per month, which means a $60 monthly increase. You're locked into the lease for a year, so that's an additional $720 you need to pay. You might move to avoid that rent hike.

Now imagine you're also renting a self-storage unit. It's convenient and among the nicest in the area. The staff is pleasant, but you don't care about that because you rarely stop by. You're paying $100 per month, and you get a notice that your rent is going up by 6 percent. Are you going to spend a Saturday renting a U-Haul, recruiting a few reluctant friends, and braving the heat or cold to move your stuff down the street just to save $6 per month—especially when most self-storage facilities don't lock you into a lease and you can typically leave any month you want to?

Highly doubtful, particularly when you think, "I'll probably only need this unit a few more months anyway. I've got to block out time to go clean that junk out of there. Maybe I'll do it on my vacation." (Or next year. Or next decade.) See the point? Self-storage tenants are sticky. And they're likely to tolerate a few rent increases annually.

Unlike apartment dwellers, they don't fraternize, so they can't compare rents. They won't know that the neighboring unit got an introductory rate that is three rent increases lower than theirs in a one-time deal. This is like airline or hotel pricing. An obvious goal for a marketer is to lure in self-storage tenants to get their attention. Ironically, when you acquire a tenant, one of the goals is to have them forget about you. Set up automatic payments, and hope they don't think about you often.

Check out this graphic showing how often self-storage tenants visit their unit.

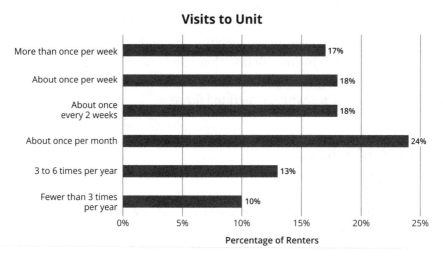

Visits to Unit

Source: SS Demand Study 2020

Many people wonder how long tenants stay at storage facilities. It varies widely. Following are the results of one study:

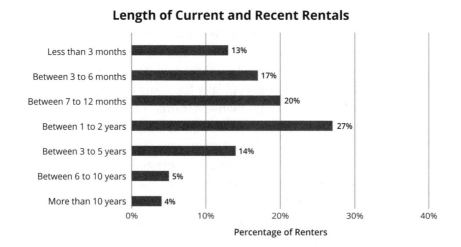

Length of Current and Recent Rentals

Source: SS Demand Study 2020

Good Performance in Recessions *and* Booms

The tenants are sticky, prices can be raised, operations and marketing can be upgraded, and equity is leveraged by income and positioning. But what about the upcoming recession? (There is always one around the corner. We just don't know when—or how severe.) Wellings Capital specifically chose self-storage, in part, because of its recession resistance.

In good times people are filling up their carts at Amazon and Walmart. Americans have more stuff than they can possibly use, and our credit card balances and low savings rates prove it. Baby boomers and their parents are downsizing or passing into the next life, and their kids want to let go of the antiques and the memories. The e-commerce economy is booming, and online entrepreneurs have sprung up across the fruited plain. Many need a place to house their inventory. America is increasingly a nation of renters, and renters often need to store stuff. For a relatively small percentage of their income, they can do that at a self-storage facility.

In bad times people are tightening their belts and cutting costs. Thankfully, self-storage is a relatively small cost in the scheme of things. Some homeowners with 4,000-square-foot houses are downsizing to 2,000-square-foot houses. Some in 2,000-square-foot houses are downsizing to apartments. And some in one- to two-bedroom apartments are moving into studio apartments or mobile homes.

In each of these cases, people need a place to store their treasures, and self-storage is the obvious answer. This proved true in the Great Recession, and it's proven true overall in the mostly good economic times these past four or five decades. Though the following graphics refer only to REIT performance, they will give you an idea of what I'm talking about.

According to the National Association of REITs (NAREIT), the self-storage sector outperformed most other real estate sectors in the recent recession. From 2007 to 2009, it produced an average of about –3.4 percent. Negative returns may not be ideal, but even apartment REITs—which performed better than residential, industrial, office, and retail—averaged –6.7 percent in that same period. For comparison, here are the returns from the other REIT sectors over that same time period. Please keep in mind that REIT returns are significantly impacted by the market as a whole, the mood of investors, and other factors that don't impact smaller operators.

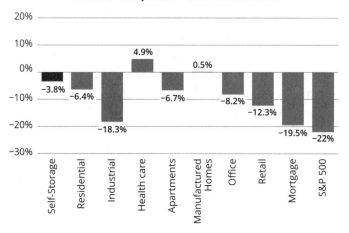

Average Annual Return by REIT Sector vs. S&P 500, 2007–2009 Recession

Source: NAREIT, https://dgydj.com/sp-500-return-calculator/

For a longer time span, check out this graphic. (Take note, stock market investors!)

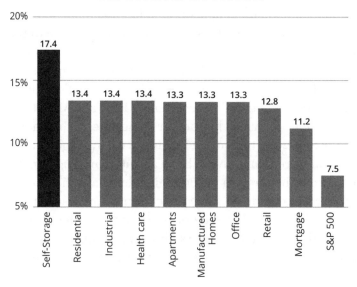

Average Annual Return by REIT Sector vs S&P 500 from 1994 to 2017

Source: NAREIT, https://dgydj.com/sp-500-return-calculator/

Ancillary Income Opportunities

There are many ways to add income and value to self-storage facilities. Self-storage is both a real estate and a retail business. Many mom-and-pop owners who operate their facilities as a passive real estate parcel don't operate a showroom. This hurts marketability in so many ways.

By adding a stylish showroom, best-in-class operators have an office, a clean place to meet with tenants, and a place to sell them more stuff. The showroom should be professionally staged and decorated to give the prospective tenant a warm feeling about whom they're doing business with and where their treasures will be housed. It should have multiple live camera views of the property and should speak of security and safety to the tenant.

Here's an example of what not to do: I was price shopping and walked into a competitor's showroom. There was a maintenance golf cart parked just inside the door. After squeezing my way past that, I suddenly thought I was in the wrong place: it looked like the interior of a mechanic's garage. They were selling a few retail items, but these were buried behind mounds of stuff.

QUICK INSIGHTS

Styling Your Storage Spaces

Not only should the showroom be stylish, well lit, and secure, but the indoor climate-controlled areas should be as well. Finding yourself alone in a long corridor of storage units can feel eerie, and having well-lit hallways and cameras in every direction provides a feeling of security. Indoor areas should look nothing like a cave.

Outdoor areas should be well lit also. Modern lighting technology and motion sensors will lower your costs and still provide great lighting inside and out.

Your self-storage facility will have the opportunity to sell all kinds of necessary items to your prospective tenants and to the public at large. Many tenants and others need:

- Boxes
- Tape
- Bubble wrap

- Scissors
- Locks
- Rental dollies and carts

In addition, think of any items—coffee mugs, baseball caps, fridge magnets—of local interest that could be marketed to locals or those who are moving to the area. And, of course, everyone needs snacks when they're moving. Here is a breakdown of popular ancillary items according to the 2020 SSA demand survey.

Items Rented or Purchased from Facility

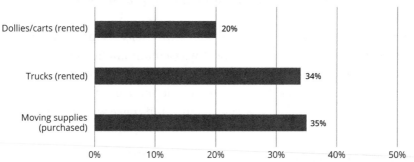

You could also provide other profitable services from your self-storage facility, especially if you have a smaller facility and are trying to justify hiring a full-time manager. A few examples include:
- Propane filling station
- eBay pack-and-ship station
- ATM
- Cell tower lease
- Billboard rentals

Other Low-Cost Value-Adds

Many self-storage value-adds cost little or nothing to implement. Some result from a mere change to policies and procedures and can often be carried out within weeks of acquiring a facility. They include:
- Implementation of administration fees
- Implementation of late fees
- Timely evictions

- Fees for paying by cash or check (small discount to pay by ACH)
- Implementation of moving truck rental (U-Haul or Penske)

As I mentioned earlier, the implementation of truck rentals costs almost nothing in most cases (other than employee time and parking spaces) and can generate up to $3,000 or more per month in revenue. It can also lead to increased occupancy of up to 3 to 5 percent. ("Would you like a storage unit with that U-Haul rental?")

QUICK INSIGHTS

U-Haul Value-Adds

A friend of mine has a facility in Rockledge, Florida. It is in a particularly well-positioned storage location. When I was there some time ago, his manager told me they had just hit the $5,000-per-month level in monthly U-Haul commission. Even with no impact on occupancy, that could translate to an increased facility value of over $900,000 and a much greater impact to the investors' equity (due to leverage).

My friend achieved this with no capital outlay. A signed contract with U-Haul, some employee training, and a few policy and procedure changes were all it took. "How can this be?" I'm glad you asked. You'll have to wait until the next chapter for the answer.

Low Operating Costs

Self-storage has one of the lowest cost structures among commercial real estate asset classes. It is fairly predictable, and with no toilets, water lines, or other nuisances, it is well suited for operators who want to minimize hassle and expense.

While there are many improvements you can make in taking a mom-and-pop operation up to a professionally run facility, operating costs are not always among them. Of course, there are exceptions, such as when the owner is paying his lazy nephew to run the place while he sits on the beach. In general, the costs associated with running a professional operation usually exceed those of a mom-and-pop, but the profit and value created far exceed those costs.

Here is a breakdown and comparison of the cost structure and profitability of commercial real estate in general with self-storage.

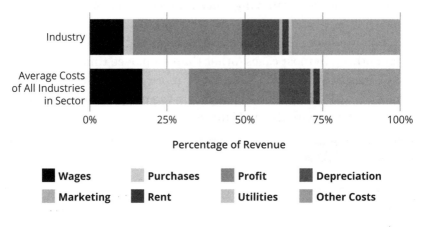

Cost Structure 2020

Percentage of Revenue

Wages Purchases Profit Depreciation

Marketing Rent Utilities Other Costs

Source: IBISWorld

Lenders Love Self-Storage

It is widely known that lenders love to provide debt for self-storage facilities. Lender Neal Gussis published an article, "Eyes Wide Open: 4 Reasons Why Lenders Are Actively Pursuing Self-Storage Investments," in *Inside Self-Storage* detailing why in 2018.[20]

According to Gussis, commercial mortgage brokers regularly get calls from lenders these days saying they're overallocated on multifamily and want to do more self-storage transactions. He claims, "It's a well-known fact that the storage industry has had the lowest default rate of all CMBS (commercial mortgage-backed securities) commercial property types for more than twenty years." Gussis goes on to explain that storage has fared much better than other commercial property types during recessionary periods but has proven strong during good economic times as well. In his view, the following are four key reasons why lenders love self-storage:

1. **Diversification.** Self-storage provides a diversified mix of renters, which mitigates credit risk of losing significant revenue from a few large tenants. Additionally, tenants have a wide variety of reasons for renting and are a mix of commercial and residential users.

2. **Lending exposure:** After decades of exposure to this relatively new

---

20 Neal Gussis, "Eyes Wide Open: 4 Reasons Why Lenders Are Actively Pursuing Self-Storage Investments," *Inside Self-Storage*, last updated May 23, 2018, https://www.insideselfstorage.com/financing/eyes-wide-open-4-reasons-why-lenders-are-actively-pursuing-self-storage-investments.

asset class, lenders are aware of the low default rates and predictable occupancy trends of self-storage borrowers.

3. **Underwriting**: Compared to other commercial real estate assets, storage facilities require fewer physical improvements and are operationally less complex. There's no need to assess lease expirations and account for planned buildup of reserves for tenant improvements and leasing expenses. Addressing tenant turnover is routine and requires little to no capital.

4. **The need for space**: While owners of other types of commercial property are grappling with finding new ways to lease their space due to changes in how people shop, work, and live, self-storage is thriving because its underlying fundamental needs are consistent.

The Role of Technology

When I first got into self-storage, I assumed that the way to beat independent operators was to install high-tech equipment, such as rental kiosks that rent you a unit and give you a receipt to present somewhere for your box purchase, and hire an outsourced phone team in the Philippines to replace your manager. While the addition of technology is great and there are many ways to benefit from it, eliminating staff is not often beneficial.

Though many millennials rent units from the parking lot by phone then walk into the showroom, many others want the security of talking to a real person. We're talking about their family heirlooms or other items of value, and they want to ask questions and know that someone real is watching over their possessions.

In fact, much of the marketing for top-flight operators is done by a human being reaching out into the community. Computers cannot attend real estate agent happy hours and meet with local moving companies to drum up business. But technology does benefit self-storage when it comes to things like smartphone-controlled gate codes and unit locks. These reduce theft and help operators catch crooks after the fact. There may also be a role for kiosks, smartphone leases, or other technology to lease units after hours or on weekends. Check out the technology options offered at www.CallPotential.com and www.OpenTechAlliance.com.

Automation

Ross Stryker is a prolific self-storage investor from Missouri. Management costs at his Birmingham, Alabama, self-storage facility were killing profits, so Ross and his team decided to replace the onsite staff with technology. He had originally accepted a bid of 100,000 annually for two site managers plus overhead from a national third-party property management firm. The management firm also shared in the insurance revenue.

Now, Ross is using Janus's Nokē (think "no key") technology, which can prevent delinquent tenants from accessing their units at an unmanned facility. In addition, a white-collar manager is handsomely compensated to manage the facility and 11 others from a central command center. The manager answers questions, takes payments, unlocks gates, and much more from the home office during business hours and is also reachable after hours for calls routed through their after-hours call center.

Ross is incurring an up-front cost of $220,000 for the technology to replace the management company. He estimates that by year five his NOI will have improved by over $100,000, from about $725,000 to $846,000. This includes the elimination of the two employees plus insurance premiums and more. At a 6 percent cap rate, this translates to an increased sale value of just over $2 million.

The previous five-year internal rate of return (IRR) on this project was projected at 14.5 percent, which was unacceptable for investors based on the risk of a ground-up, two-phase project. The new IRR projection after implementing technology is 21 percent.

This seems to be a case where missing out on additional income items like retail sales (locks, boxes, tape, and scissors) will be worthwhile. I originally wondered whether they would miss out on anything else by going virtual. Apparently not too much: Ross just updated me and said they are leasing up the facility at 9 percent per month. That's nearly three times what they expected.

Ross believes that artificial intelligence and automation will eventually become standard in self-storage just as it has in so many industries. He predicts that we will soon be getting packages via drones and driving next to driverless semi-trucks, pointing out that we already order from computers at McDonald's and pay at self-checkouts at the grocery store. Why wouldn't we rent storage in the same way?

Ross's Birmingham facility is evidence he may be right. On the other hand, a few other firms we invest with argue that marketing can never be outsourced to a computer, and that is too valuable to miss—at least for them.

Earlier I alluded to the powerful role of technology in understanding customer motivations and setting rents accordingly. A smart operator will take advantage of such revenue management tools. You may not like the pricing policies of hotels and airlines whereby some customers pay much more than others, but you'll be glad to have this technology to maximize your income and occupancy. If you don't, the REIT down the street will.

Revenue management software can also help you determine optimization of unit sizes and even variable pricing for ground versus upper floors, location within the facility, time of year, and more. Think of it as a highly experienced manager with a genius-level IQ and a perfect memory working for you 24/7.

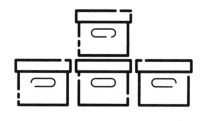

CHAPTER 3

THE WINNING PROFIT AND VALUE FORMULA

Let's talk about big-picture investment strategy. You know that Babe Ruth was considered baseball's home run king. He held records for decades, and he's a legend in American sports. Did you know that he was also a strikeout king? The Babe led the American League in strikeouts five times. His all-or-nothing style led to his immense popularity and fame. Should you invest the way Babe Ruth played?

As an employee turned entrepreneur turned investor, I certainly thought so. It was exciting to hear stories of $1,000 turned into millions or a random idea turned into a multinational corporation. But, as a whole, those strategies are not the way to build a great real estate empire or investing career.

So far, I've made the case that commercial self-storage investing has compelling demographic, financial, and operational drivers that have captured the attention of many investors. The risk-return profile is also surprisingly strong.

Risk and Return

Complete this two-part sentence with the first thing that pops into your head: Low risk leads to low return; high risk leads to _ _ _ _ return.

You've probably already figured out where I'm going here. It is so natural to think that high risk leads to high return. As entrepreneurs, and as Americans, we are generally an optimistic bunch.

We look at a full range of potential outcomes, and we want to believe the best one will come to pass. This is the stuff that most entrepreneurs are made of. This is what led Thomas Edison to obtain 1,093 patents and Sir Richard Branson to control more than 400 companies. But high risk does not lead to high return. High risk leads to the *potential* for high return—and the potential for low or zero return as well.

Risk-Return Tradeoff

Source: Investopedia.com

Higher risk may lead to higher returns... and it may lead to higher losses. Including the loss of all your principal.

This is where a lot of entrepreneurs get into trouble. And I want to spare you from this potential pitfall if I can. I call it the *entrepreneurial investment trap*.

The Entrepreneurial Investment Trap

Have you succeeded as an entrepreneur? Good for you if so! But you may want to consider the possibility that the way you succeeded as an entrepreneur may not help you prosper as an investor. Let me explain. Though this is not universally true, it is often the case that entrepreneurs take significant risks to reach an uncertain outcome.

Take Jeff Bezos for example. Let's say it's late 1995 and Bezos is your new neighbor. He greets you from the driveway of his rented Seattle area house while you're walking your dog. Your casual inquiry about what he's got going on in that garage all hours leads to his passionate 15-minute explanation about his dream to sell books and become a major book retailer. Out of his garage. He's going to call it Amazon.com.

You may have asked what he means by selling *online*. And you may have smiled kindly and walked away shaking your head about his nutty strategy. And what in the heck does *dot com* mean anyway?

Would you have guessed he would be the wealthiest man in the world in a little over two decades? Bezos took a dream and made it into reality through his entrepreneurial efforts.

His parents' $250,000 initial investment paid off, too. They're reportedly worth north of $30 billion today. Jeff had warned his parents and initial investors there was a 70 percent chance they would lose their money. (Reflecting on it today, I can't imagine that the risk was that low.)

Bezos's story is epic. It's told and retold and will be for the rest of our lives and beyond. His story is famous in part because it's an exception. Entrepreneurial successes are a statistical minority. The Bureau of Labor Statistics tells us that about approximately 65 percent of businesses will fail during the first 10 years.[21]

Years ago, as I looked over the many business cards in my drawer, I wondered if I should get a new one with the title "serial entrepreneur" on it. That's how I thought of myself. This mindset became part of who I was—but this mindset didn't serve me well when I became an investor. The high stakes, high risk/high *potential* return lifestyle seemed like breathing to me, so I brought it into my investing strategy.

It seemed reasonable to me to throw a lot of money down a hole in the ground in an unproven location with the hope it would produce 10 or 100 times as much in oil revenues. (It produced zero.) And when an

---

21 U.S. Bureau of Labor Statistics. "Table 7. Survival of private sector establishment by opening year." https://www.bls.gov/bdm/us_age_naics_00_table7.txt

alternative financial planner told me about a "cool" strategy to make easy passive income, I bit on that apple, too. (It was rotten at its core.) And there was that retired military guy who sold me his pension stream in exchange for my cash. (I'm still not sure how he got it back by declaring bankruptcy two years later.)

Any of these *could* have worked out fine. But as an investor, I don't want to gamble with my hard-earned investment funds. Again, it's important to remember that high risk does not lead to high return. It leads to high **potential** return. Equally true is that it leads to high **potential** loss. You need to invest in deals where the principals will never gamble with your assets. And if you're the principal, you will certainly want to be that type of person on behalf of your investors.

I know so many people who've done this wrong. After a big initial success, they find themselves chasing that elusive goal through many frustrating years and failures. While that may be fun for your entrepreneurial journey, I hope you will put on a different hat for your investing journey.

Paul Samuelson, who was the first American to win the Nobel Prize in economics, said: "Investing should be like watching paint dry or watching grass grow. If you want excitement, take $800 and go to Las Vegas."

Investing versus Speculating

I wish I'd known the difference earlier in my life. As I said in the introduction chapter, investing is when your principal is generally safe and you have a chance to make a return. Speculating is when your principal is not at all safe and you have a chance to make a return. Though the distinction is not always clear up front, I urge you to consider *investing* with the bulk of your capital. If you want to speculate, go ahead, but realize that you are swinging for the fences. I recommend that you only speculate with funds that you are completely willing to lose. Then, if you make a profit on these funds, great!

Is there a measurable and predictable cash flow stream being thrown off by the asset? If so, this is an indicator of true, quantifiable value and that this is an investment rather than a speculation. Think of the three investments I mentioned earlier in the book. These assets were buoyed up to crazy extremes through wild optimism:

- Tulip bulbs
- Late 90s tech stocks
- Bitcoin

There are so many more examples. Did you notice that each of these three had no measurable, predictable income stream? Their value was driven by speculation.

Predictable income stream is one of the things I love about commercial real estate. This is why many of the smartest and most successful investors on the planet invest this way. Recall our formula that drives a quantifiable value for commercial real estate assets:

$$\text{Value} = \frac{\text{Net Operating Income}}{\text{Cap Rate}}$$

Though some of the strategies for generating significant wealth in commercial real estate involve a degree of speculation, overall, commercial real estate is a realm that provides investors with a fairly predictable, measurable income stream and, therefore, a quantifiable value. In other words, it's an investment.

So what does risk and return really look like with self-storage?

20-Year Return/Risk Profile Across Major Asset Classes

Source: Thomson Reuters Datastream, Data from 1993 to 2013

If you have invested in any of the asset classes in this graphic, then this should be of particular interest. I know it's not easy to decipher at a glance, but if you're a smart investor—and I know you are, since you're reading this book—your goal is to be as high as possible on the return axis and as low as possible on the risk/volatility axis. In other words, you want to be in the upper-left part of the chart.

Take a close look. Note that core commercial real estate has by far the best risk-adjusted returns of the major asset classes. This analysis applies to all core commercial real estate. The risk-adjusted returns of self-storage, manufactured housing, and multifamily shine brightly within this class, making the case for these three sectors even more compelling.

The Sharpe Ratio is a measurement of the risk-adjusted return for investments. The goal, of course, is to get the highest return per "unit of risk." Return by itself is an inadequate predictor of a good investment. Correlating both returns and risk (as measured by value instability) is a sounder way of comparing opportunities.

The following table compares the Sharpe Ratios for a variety of different asset types in the commercial real estate realm. As you can see, the Sharpe Ratio for self-storage is a full 33% stronger than the next closest asset types.

Key Performance Statistics Of U.S. Equity REIT Subsector Based on Total Returns Jan 1994–Dec 2015, Sorted by Sharpe Ratio (Highest to Lowest)

	Sharpe Ratio	Annualized STDDev, %	Annualized Return, %
Self-Storage	0.8	19.6	17.6
Fr-Stand	0.6	17.7	13.0
Apartments	0.6	19.8	12.4
Office	0.5	21.5	11.2
Reg Malls	0.5	25.9	13.3
Manufactured	0.5	18.2	11.4
HealthCare	0.5	20.7	12.3
FNUSERI	0.5	19.7	10.7
Industrial	0.4	30.5	8.8
ShopCtr	0.4	21.9	10.2
Diversified	0.4	20.9	8.7
Lodge-Res	0.2	30.5	4.6

Source: FTSE Russell, NAREIT, data as of 31 December 2015.

The Four Pillars of Return in Commercial Real Estate

I bet you're thinking to yourself, *You are trumpeting the marvelous returns and limited downside of the self-storage sector. How are those returns derived?* Well, ROI is derived from four components, known as CAPT for short:

C = Cash Return
A = Appreciation
P = Principal Paydown
T = Tax Benefits

Cash Return

This return is derived from the free cash flow of the property. As an investor in commercial self-storage, it's likely that your cash returns will be higher—sometimes quite a bit higher—than the taxable income on your K-1. We'll get into that more in the tax chapter (chapter 4).

Of course, this will vary widely, but for the purpose of this book, here's a very rough estimate on how your cash returns could shake out based on $100 of gross operating income.

Gross Income	$100
Less Operating Expenses	$34
Net Income	**$66**
Less Capital Reserves	$4
Less Asset Management Fee	$2
Free Cash Flow	**$60**

Without getting any deeper into the weeds, let's just say that this free cash flow represents a 7 percent return on the value of the asset (ROA). That doesn't sound overly exciting, right?

But the return on equity (ROE), with equity being the cash invested, is much higher. Why? Safe leverage. If the total debt as a fraction of the asset value is two-thirds (66.7 percent LTV), then the cash invested will be only one-third of the asset value, so the cash-on-cash ROE for this example would be about 12 percent.

Gross Income	$100
Less Operating Expenses	$34
Net Income	**$66**
Less Capital Reserves	$4
Less Loan Principal and Interest	$26
Less Asset Management Fee	$2
Free Cash Flow	**$34**

Typical cash-on-cash returns for profitable self-storage assets are between 3 and 7 percent early on, and perhaps about 12 percent or more later in the ownership period. But that's not all you get!

Appreciation

The value of a stabilized commercial asset is generally the NOI divided by the cap rate. While both numbers are subject to some market forces beyond the operator's/investor's control, there are many factors that are controllable through careful planning and execution. This is where I think value-add projects shine as a subclass of the self-storage sector. Since appreciation is a function of both NOI and cap rate, both will be described in detail in this chapter.

Improving NOI is based on increasing rental income and other income while hopefully maintaining or decreasing operating costs as a percentage of income. Value-add properties provide an opportunity for the new owner to achieve a disproportionately high ROI on capital and management improvements made to the property. This may be derived from a long list of factors, but a few examples include increasing rents, occupancy, and other income by:

- improving the property's interior and exterior appearance and functionality;
- increasing the effectiveness of marketing;
- adding new self-storage buildings (typically climate-controlled, since older assets often have more non-climate-controlled buildings);
- adding or improving revenue sources, such as truck rental, late fees, administration fees, and insurance sales; or
- adding or improving a showroom with point-of-sale (POS) items like locks, boxes, tape, and scissors.

NOI may also be improved by reducing expenses. A good asset manager and property manager will have dozens of ways to achieve this. Examples of expense categories to manage include:

- Payroll and benefits
- Property taxes
- Insurance
- Utilities
- Administration and management expenses
- Repairs and maintenance
- Marketing expenditures

As I mentioned earlier, I don't typically recommend a strategy that is hyper-focused on expense reduction at the expense of a full range of services. There is a place for automation, but trying to eliminate staff at a medium-to-large facility will often reduce net income overall.

Now that we've talked about the role of NOI in driving appreciation, let's move on to cap rate. Your cap rate represents the market's evaluation of your unleveraged yield for that asset class in that market. Integra Realty Resources (www.IRR.com) states that the cap rate is driven by these seven factors:

1. Supply and demand
2. Property income growth
3. Local economy, job growth, and unemployment
4. National economic conditions and GDP growth
5. Interest rates
6. Availability of financing
7. Risk premium of private real estate

Our team generally likes to invest in markets where cap rates vary from about 6 to 8 percent. Cap rates on the lower end of the spectrum (higher-priced asset purchases) can be managed by aggressive rent growth in the first few years and through interest-only loans (typically available for up to three to five years).

Metropolitan statistical areas (MSAs) with very low cap rates (*expensive!*), such as New York City, San Francisco, and Chicago, usually don't generate much cash flow during the first few years of the investment. Institutional investors like insurance companies and REITs can handle this type of return profile because they realize it may translate to very steady yields in later years. Lower-cap-rate markets are expensive but typically more stable. Buyers in these areas are willing to pay a premium for this predictability.

Low cap rates do not necessarily speak to the health of a market as much as they indicate its stability. For the typical investor, ultra-low-cap-rate markets don't make as much sense as moderate-rate markets. What about high-cap-rate markets? Should you celebrate the opportunity to buy in a 9 percent cap market? Maybe, but not necessarily. These markets can sometimes experience the widest swings in value.

Of course, it is possible to get a higher cap rate (lower price) on an individual asset based on a number of risk factors. Especially in times of economic decline or uncertainty, there may be opportunities to purchase an asset at a high cap rate. This cap rate could swing wildly in the positive direction based on the asset manager's ability to turn the property around quickly.

Let's take a second to see what this kind of cap rate could mean to investors. A 1,000-unit property with a NOI of $1.2 million in a 7 percent cap rate economy would be valued at about $17.1 million ($1.2 million / 7 percent; I'll explain this further later in this chapter). However, the same property at the same net income would be valued at $21.8 million if cap rates tightened to 5.5 percent, so even if the owner did nothing to improve the property and its income, its value would go up substantially. Of course, investing in value-add properties means you will be taking aggressive actions to improve the property, the rents, and the net income, regardless of the market. The value-adds can often more than compensate for a negative move in cap rate.

In this example, the change in value is contingent on a change in the economy based on the particulars of a specific market. Note that the first three of the seven cap rate factors listed above are mostly local in nature, while the last four are more national in scope.

What impact could a change like the one in the example above have on the value of the investors' equity? Remember that income was held constant, but the cap rate changed from 7 to 5.5 percent. (This can happen through economic factors or by improving the asset to sell to a REIT as mentioned in chapter 2.) The value of *the asset* moved from $17.1 to $21.8 million, a healthy 27.5 percent increase in asset value.

The value to the investors is significantly magnified by leverage. If this property has 60 percent leverage (LTV), which is generally considered a safe level, you can multiply the return on asset (ROA) by 2.5 to get the return on equity (ROE).

The math on this is:

$$\frac{\text{ROA} \times 1}{(1 - \text{LTV})} = \text{multiplier to get from ROA to ROE}$$

so

$$\frac{\text{ROA} \times 1}{(1 - 0.6)} = 2.5$$

so

$$\underset{(\text{ROA})}{27.5\%} \times \underset{(\text{multiplier})}{2.5} = \underset{(\text{ROE})}{68.75\%}$$

To calculate the impact on investor equity, multiply the 27.5 percent increase in asset value (ROA) by 2.5, and the appreciation to equity (ROE) is over 68 percent—just from the change in cap rate! Do you see why smart value-add operators want to acquire assets that can be improved and sold to REITs and other institutional buyers? Do you see the power of investing in a down market that is on the rise?

QUICK INSIGHTS

Rentability

We've discussed the role of income and expenses in driving appreciation. One more category that deserves mention is rentability. This is a subjective category that is harder to quantify but nonetheless important. Rentability may not directly result in the opportunity to raise rents—and it may not result in any cost savings—but it is likely to increase occupancy and tenant retention, therefore the overall income and value of the property.

Rentability can often be improved by bringing in a great property management team. That can be as simple as hiring a great property manager who possesses stellar character and great sales skills. Character cannot be taught but is a function of who the person is. Sales skills, on the other hand, can be learned and improved upon.

Some of the factors driving increased rentability include:

- Professionalism
- Dependability/follow-through
- Convenience
- Aesthetics
- Perceived safety and security
- Service

Principal Paydown

Principal paydown is pretty simple and may not even sound as if it should be part of the return. It is cash flow that could have been distributed to the investors but instead is used to increase equity along the way. Your storage tenants pay down your mortgage while you sleep, and you do nothing special to achieve this benefit.

Principal paydown is a legitimate part of your return because the money spent to pay down the mortgage is cash returns that owner-investors are forgoing year in and year out. If there were no paydown, as in the first few years of an interest-only product, this cash would go straight to the distributable cash bucket to be enjoyed by investors.

This kicks in after any interest-only period ends (if applicable). The increase in equity typically amounts to a substantial return. As an investor, you won't see any benefit from this in your quarterly distribution, but you will experience this benefit at the time of debt refinance or the sale of the property.

We once reviewed a Dallas, Texas, multifamily property with 586 units. The estimated price was about $55,000 per unit, or $32,230,000 total. We would have invested $8,125,000 in cash (equity) and financed $24,375,000 (a 10-year commercial loan with a 30-year amortization schedule at 4 percent interest).

Principal paydown started at $434,609 in year one and totals $5,217,958 over the 10-year term. When dividing principal paydown by equity, the return is 5.3 percent for full year one and progresses to 7.6 percent annually by year 10. This is a cumulative return on invested capital of $5.2 million ÷ $8.125 million = 64.2 percent, or 6.42 percent annually, which is a nice addition to the returns for investors at the time of refinance or sale.

Tax Benefits

"If the American public knew how little we're taxed, we'd have a revolt on our hands!" said a friend of mine before launching into an explanation of how he and his investors could parlay $20 million cash into a $210 million commercial real estate portfolio over two decades, pocket $131 million along the way, and pay virtually no taxes—all in complete compliance with the tax code.

This subject is so important that I've dedicated the entire next chapter to covering taxes in detail. You can check out a full menu of tax benefits from commercial real estate there.

The Value Equation: Putting It All Together

While this book is about self-storage, the key takeaways from this book also apply to manufactured housing, multifamily, and all types of commercial real estate. This is the reason that most of the Forbes 400, the wealthiest of the wealthy, made their money in commercial real estate or are buying it to sustain and propagate their wealth. This is what I tell anyone who'll listen: *If I had known about the power of commercial real estate to grow my income and increase my wealth, I would never have done anything else.*

As I mentioned earlier, commercial real estate is valued differently than residential real estate. Residential real estate is valued based on comparable properties. No matter how nicely you fix up your home, its value will still be limited by the value of the other homes in the neighborhood. Commercial real estate values, however, are based on math. The value equation for commercial real estate is:

$$\text{Value} = \frac{\textbf{Net Operating Income}}{\textbf{Cap Rate}}$$

Buyers of stabilized commercial real estate are buying an income stream. Yes, they're also buying bricks and sticks and sheet metal and rivets. But their focus is the income stream.

(By the way, they may pay a premium for income potential. In other words, if you have additional land or perhaps storage buildings that were just built and are not yet leased, you should get a value assigned for those as well, but this is the exception to the general formula.)

What are your marching orders to increase the value of your commercial real estate asset?

Increase the Numerator and Compress the Denominator in the Value Equation.

It's that straightforward! Let's put it all together with an example.

A Real-Life Example

Many of the assets I invest in have a nice value-add component. This is often the result of a prior mom-and-pop operator who didn't have the desire or resources to optimize income and drive values up. This particular example provided many fortunate opportunities for upgrades, and while the upgrades are fairly typical for a great operator, the outcome was better than most.

It was a self-storage facility in Beeville, Texas, which is a small town, but the population and demographics support the business. And there is virtually no threat from a national player building a competitive facility nearby.

This acquisition was sourced through a phone call to one of the owners. Our operating partner visited the facility and learned that it had been recently inherited by five siblings who were fighting and eager to sell as soon as possible. It was not run well, and the value was significantly below its potential and getting even worse as its management eroded.

Our operating partner offered $2.4 million for the property, and they closed in March 2019 for cash at this price. This was a fair price considering the situation. He later learned that it had been on the market with a local commercial broker for more than $5 million. The broker was not casting a wide net, and the price was far out of line with the value given its poor management.

Here are a few highlights...

- This facility, built in 1999, consisted of 607 non-climate-controlled units with 75,000 net rentable square feet.
- The owners claimed occupancy of 91 percent, but upon reviewing financials, the buyer discovered that more than 60 units were seriously delinquent on payments. This dropped the effective occupancy by about 10 percent to a new total of 81 percent.
- This was a classic case of mismanagement. There was no internet

marketing, excessive expenses, significantly below-market rents, and a lack of customer service skills that are necessary in a small town like Beeville.

At the time of acquisition, the property had a gross monthly income potential (at current rental rates and occupancy but not counting delinquency) of $27,000. At the four-month mark, the new operator had maintained existing occupancy, eliminated all past due tenants via auctions, and increased the gross potential monthly income to $39,000.

Here are some of the value-adds:

- The addition of U-Haul rentals added $500 to the monthly income at virtually no cost to the company.
- Two rent increases totaling 20 to 30 percent were implemented within the first several months of ownership.
- The decrease in delinquency added more than 10 percent to the top line revenue and about 13 percent to the net operating income.
- A showroom was added to the facility. This provided a better customer experience and an opportunity to sell ancillary items like locks, boxes, tape, and scissors.
- A website and an online marketing program were implemented to support all of these initiatives.

Within the first six months of ownership, the operator got an appraisal for $4.6 million. This is nearly double the value at acquisition just months earlier! The operator then put debt of about $2 million on the property (at a 43 percent LTV on the new value), meaning only about $400,000 in the original cash was left in the project.

How is this possible? Was this a once-in-a-lifetime event, or something that can be replicated by this operator and others? The key to success was finding a well-located asset that was under-managed and fairly priced, then implementing easy value-adds.

Let's look at the potential impact of a few of these items. Since this property was acquired for cash and financed later, the return to the investors was unusually high. For the sake of this example, however, I would like to assume a more typical loan-to-cost at an acquisition of 60 percent, then I will circle back and tell you how the numbers actually turned out. These numbers assume a steady cap rate for simplicity.

- Increasing rents by an average of 25 percent will increase profits substantially, perhaps by 30 percent or more since operational costs generally don't increase. The effect on the value of the asset is about 30 percent (easy math: Value = Income / Cap Rate). However, the effect on equity investors is much higher due to leverage. With an LTV of about 60 percent, the impact to equity appreciation is 30 percent / (1 − 0.60) = 75 percent. (At 60 percent LTV leverage, the impact on equity is 2.5x the impact on asset value, as we discussed earlier.)

- Decreasing delinquency by 10 percent increases income by about 13 percent—since expenses don't rise with increased rents, the net operating income grows more than just the revenues. This increases asset value by 13 percent and boosts equity by more than 32 percent. (A 13 percent increase in net operating income leads directly to a 13 percent increase in value. Multiply that number by 2.5x due to leverage to get 32 percent.)
- There is also increased income from point of sale items, U-Haul, marketing improvements, and more. Assume increased NOI of 4 percent from all of this. This impacts the asset value by 4 percent, and the equity value by 10 percent (again, we multiply by 2.5x due to leverage).
- Decreasing inflated operating expenses by 20 percent resulted in an increased NOI of about 25 percent (since expenses were held constant and revenues rose). This led to an increased value of 25 percent and an increase to equity of 62.5 percent (again the NOI increase matches the value increase, and the leverage raises the return on equity by 2.5x).

There are other ways the operator could increase income and value—but assuming he successfully completed the projects above (he did), the combined *asset appreciation* from the four changes above is 78 percent (30 + 13 + 10 + 25 percent).

When applying "normal" leverage on this, this could arguably result in an equity appreciation of 195 percent. That's 78 percent / (1 − 0.60) = 195 percent. In our real-life example, the equity appreciation far exceeded this as you'll soon find out.

A Note on Cap Rates

In this case, since the property was performing poorly, the acquisition cap rate was more compressed than might have been justified if optimally run. Sometimes great operators will do this when there is significant upside potential.

There are many times when this is not the case. You may be able to acquire a property at a 7 percent cap rate, for example, and sell it for a more compressed cap rate (say 5.5 percent, which is a typical rate for many sales these days). If you can buy at a 7 percent cap rate and sell at a 5.5 percent cap rate, this is a 27 percent increase in value in itself. (Dividing the same income by 0.055 versus 0.070 will result in a 27 percent-plus higher sales price.) When multiplied by the leverage effect in our example [27 percent / (1 – 0.60)], this could result in an increase of about 68 percent in the value of the equity—all without increasing the net operating income or changing anything else.

Recall that our value formula is based on CAPT. We just focused on the A in CAPT, which is appreciation. Let's also remember that investors will receive cash flow and principal paydown in a deal like this as well. In this case, the stabilized cash flow averaged well over 10 percent (return on equity) annually. The principal paydown is actually zero if this property is sold in the first several years since the operator got three-year, interest-only debt. It could average about 3 percent per year after that.

What is the return on equity for investors if this property is held for six years? I'll keep this scenario simple for explanation's sake. Assume 10 percent cash flow annually with no further NOI increases. Assume the cap rate is steady. Assume the principal paydown is 9 percent total after the interest-only period in the last three years. And assume the equity appreciation of 195 percent that we calculated earlier does not expand further.

What is the total return on equity on this asset?

$$\underset{\text{appreciation}}{195\%} + \underset{(6 \text{ years} \times 10\% = 60\%)}{60\% \text{ cash flow}} + \underset{\text{paydown}}{9\% \text{ principal}} = 264\%$$

$$\frac{264\%}{6 \text{ years}} = 44\% \text{ (annual return on equity)}$$

This profit is shared by the operator and equity investors, but this is no small income stream and payday for both.

Concluding This Example: What Actually Happened?

Since this is a true story, you won't be surprised to hear that this self-storage facility sold for $4.6 million. You may be surprised to know that the sale occurred without a broker only 18 months after acquisition, in September 2020. As a result of the cash purchase and quick refinance, with only about $400,000 cash left in the deal (but with higher average equity due to original cash purchase), the $2.2 million appreciation plus profit from cash flow resulted in a multiple of invested capital (MOIC) of 5.9x and an internal rate of return (IRR) of 89 percent.

This is clearly a wonderfully positive outcome. But it is repeatable. None of these operational upgrades are unusual, and some projects have more that could be added. Imagine how the value could be enhanced by adding a climate-controlled facility or boat and RV parking. Or imagine a property with a delinquency rate over 50 percent, like another self-storage facility in Colorado we invested in last year. The bottom line on this strategy is this: Our operating partner acquired this property at a very attractive valuation, brought rates to the market level, reduced expenses, and invested in their manager to execute on their strategy.

Can you replicate this type of deal? Maybe not. But one of the keys is to find a well-positioned, reasonably priced opportunity. These don't come easy. But they're out there.

Next, let's discuss the T in CAPT, the tax benefits available to commercial real estate investors.

CHAPTER 4

SELF-STORAGE TAX STRATEGIES

If you take $1 and double it daily tax-free for 20 days, it will be worth $1,048,576. Take that same $1, double it daily for 20 days but tax it every day at 30 percent, and it will be worth only $40,640—a loss of a million dollars! Why? Because with tax-free compounding, earnings accumulate not only on the principal but also on the tax-free earnings ("earnings on earnings"). Thus, compounding combines earning power on principal and earning power on interest. Compounding has been called the eighth wonder of the world, a miracle. Compounding money at high rates of tax-free return is a definite advantage of real estate, especially with a great tax plan.

Tax Strategies

Ed, a friend and fellow commercial real estate investor, told me the story of why he hired a tax strategist. As a real estate investor and real estate broker, Ed made a lot of profit over a lot of years, and he had a whopping tax bill to prove it.

He once read an article about a surprising tax-savings tip and met his CPA for lunch to share it. The CPA agreed it was a great idea and said they should implement it right away—maybe even refile for a few years to capture some of the benefits.

Somewhat irritated, Ed went on to share another tax-saving strategy he heard from a fellow investor. His CPA agreed that was also a great idea and something they should implement. After what I imagine was a long pause, Ed said, "Hold on. You're saying you knew about these tax savings strategies all along... and didn't tell me?" (That's when the pleasant lunch got tense.)

His CPA replied: "Ed, you're paying me to file your tax returns, not to be your tax strategist."

That was the last CPA/client lunch these two would ever "enjoy" together. As you can guess, Ed fired his CPA and found a new one. This one took the time to carefully analyze Ed's situation. A real estate investor himself, he had dozens of other clients in the real estate business and turned over every potential stone to minimize Ed's taxes.

The result was powerful. Ed had been paying taxes averaging about $120,000 annually for about a decade. After implementing the strategies recommended by his new tax strategist CPA, his taxes have been approximately zero in the decade since. And, yes, this was all legal and above-board.

I'm going to review some of these tax strategies in this chapter. If you're not aware of the tax strategies uniquely available to real estate investors, this could be a happy day for you.

"Over and over again the Courts have said that there is nothing sinister in so arranging affairs as to keep taxes as low as possible. Everyone does it, rich and poor alike and all do right, for nobody owes any public duty to pay more than the law demands."

—*Judge Learned Hand, Second Circuit Court of Appeals, 1947*

Direct Investment

When you buy stocks or mutual funds, you own a fraction of equity in a company. When you buy bonds, you own a fraction of debt in a company or governmental unit. When you're taxed, you will get the benefit of saving on FICA (Social Security and Medicare) since you are a passive investor, which is a nice benefit.

When you invest in real estate, assuming you do it the way I'm recommending, you will be considered a direct owner of the property. And as such, you will receive significant pass-through benefits made available in the IRS codes. These benefits could provide a paper loss or breakeven for you, though you are receiving regular checks in the mail.

You will know if you are a direct owner if you are getting a K-1 from the real estate sponsor or syndicator. If you're receiving a 1099, you will probably not enjoy full access to many of these rewarding tax benefits.

Return of Capital

Your sponsors (the operators who make the decisions about a property's operations and financials) may choose to treat certain portions of your cash flow as a return of capital, also known as "return of principal."

For example, some sponsors set a preferred return hurdle rate (often 5 to 9 percent). Passive cash investors receive all of the cash flow from the investment up to this level, and the sponsor only shares in the profits above this level. Some sponsors set up their investment to treat all of the cash flow up to this preferred return level as profit, which could be taxable, and returns above this level as "return of capital." This "excess cash flow" could be considered a return of the investor's original investment, and, therefore, not taxable until the full original investment is returned to them.

Whether the cash flow is considered a return of capital in this manner, at the time of refinance, or at another point in the life of the investment, it is obviously untaxed. As you saw in the example of doubling a dollar daily, untaxed cash flow—even if taxed down the road—can provide significant compounded returns over time.

Refinance Tax Free

Have you ever refinanced your home? How much tax did you pay on the refinance proceeds? I recently refinanced my home. I'm not only getting one of the lowest rates in history, but I'm freeing up "lazy equity" to invest in some of our company's real estate deals.

Refinancing a self-storage facility is similar to refinancing your home.

It is effectively handing your capital back to you, and it results in no tax to the operator or investors. This is a great strategy to extract some of the principal paydown and appreciation that has accumulated in the asset to use for reinvestment or otherwise.

Warning: You may be more confident in the refinance loan on an asset than you were in the original purchase loan since you're now familiar with the property. And your lender may encourage you to do a high LTV loan that may involve a bit more risk. I recommend that you continue to observe a safe debt-service coverage ratio (DSCR) and continue to maintain loan reserves. The DSCR is, in my opinion, the most important ratio in assuring that you have an adequate margin of safety in financing and operating your property. It is a great barometer of the health of your investment, and you would be wise to monitor it at every point in the investment process.

Accelerated Depreciation Through Cost Segregation

I was feeling down the other day. I am in the middle of a side deal on a self-storage property and another one on a mobile home park. These are both wholesale deals I stumbled into, so I am essentially flipping them from the seller to the end buyer/operator. I finally sat down to calculate the taxes. I was happy to learn from my tax strategist that I could avoid FICA, which is 15.3 percent up to a certain level (since I am not a dealer— wholesaling is not my business). Even so, my tax rate will be 37 percent federal plus 5.75 percent state.

I was upset to learn that over 40 percent of my profit would be swept away! After confirming I could probably not do a 1031 exchange and reviewing other non-workable options, I resigned myself to paying the tax.

Then the joyful truth hit me with full force.

Many of the tax benefits I'm trumpeting in this chapter will wipe out most (or potentially all) of my theoretically enormous tax bill for this year. And accelerated depreciation from a cost segregation study will play a major role in this. What exactly am I talking about?

Depreciation is a method for allocating the cost of an asset over its useful life. For the most part, the IRS won't allow the full write-off of the cost of a capital asset in the year of its acquisition. In general, they direct operators to space out the cost of an asset over a number of years. In the case of residential real estate, this period is 27.5 years. For commercial real estate, this period is 39 years. Since there is inherent value in the land itself, the value of the underlying land is not depreciable.

But there are a number of other shorter time categories as well, and this opens the door to this powerful strategy. The simplest way to calculate annual depreciation is to use the straight-line method. Under this method, the total depreciable value of the asset would be divided by the number of years and then applied equally as a cost on financial statements each year.

As a simple example, if you have a residential asset with a depreciable value (which doesn't include land) of $275,000, divide that figure by 27.5 years and the owner/operator would apply $10,000 annually to the income statement as the cost of this property (rather than applying the total cost in the year of purchase).

There is a major advantage to accelerating depreciation into earlier years if possible. But the default is straight-line depreciation. And this is what Ed's accountant was doing before Ed busted him. That is the easy path. Fortunately, the code allows astute operator/investors to go the extra mile to accelerate a potentially significant portion of the cost of an asset.

Why? Because there are components of a real estate asset that have a shorter useful life. And the code allows these components to be depreciated over a shorter time frame. These items will be segregated out of the value of the asset as a whole and depreciated on their own shorter schedules. This will result in larger paper losses to investors in earlier years, and lower taxable income in earlier years can be very beneficial.

How is this accomplished? The IRS likes to see detailed documentation on this. This is normally done through a comprehensive cost segregation study. This type of study is usually done by a CPA and/or engineer, and more often a specialist team including both. The study breaks out the components of the property and separates them into buckets based on their projected useful life. Then these buckets are tallied up and a depreciation schedule is applied to each group.

Here's an example. Let's say your firm acquired a self-storage facility for $4.875 million. The value is 20 percent land and 80 percent buildings, land improvements, and components. So, we subtract the land value of $975,000 from the total. If we depreciate the balance of $3.9 million, or the 20 percent of land value, on a straight-line basis, this means the operator can subtract $100,000 annually ($3.9 million / 39 years) from its net income annually. This will result in a $100,000 cost on the profit and loss statements, which leaves a lower taxable profit every year.

Now let's say the operator goes to the effort of performing a cost segregation study. The study will break out components like HVAC, cabinets, countertops, roofs, landscaping, software, hardware, electrical, windows, doors, interior storage cages, flooring, shelving, vehicles, lighting, alarms, fencing, pavement, paint, and more into shorter depreciable timelines. This study will typically be 40 to 60 pages long, but for simplicity, let's say that 25 percent of the cost of the building can be accelerated by an average of 7 years. After cost segregation, most of the acceleration goes from 39 years to either 3, 5, or 15 years, so 7 years is a reasonable weighted average.

This means that $975,000 of the $3.9 million (that is 25 percent and just happens to be the same as the land value) will be pulled out of the cost basis and be depreciated over an average of 7 years. And the remaining $2,925,000 would still be depreciated over 39 years. $975,000 / 7 = $139,286 annually. And the balance of $2,925,000, still divided by 39 years, is $75,000 annually. The combined annual depreciation for the first 7 years then is $214,286 annually, which is over double the straight-line level of $100,000 per year.

In a situation with an annual pre-depreciation income of $300,000 for example, the straight-line scenario would cover only one-third of that amount, resulting in $200,000 ($300,000 −$100,000) in taxable income. But by using cost segregation, the taxable income would drop to only $85,714 ($300,000 − $214,286) with the same cash flow into investors' pockets.

While this may sound amazing, it actually got better as a result of the 2017 tax law overhaul. All of the accelerated depreciation on a 15-year or less timeline can now be accelerated into the first year. In this example, the first 7 years of accelerated depreciation are stacked into year one. That's $139,286 × 7 = $975,002 of tax write-offs in the first year of ownership. (Yes, you read that right!)

Consider this: In a scenario with two-thirds leverage, the debt on this acquisition would be $3.25 million (two-thirds of the purchase price of $4.875 million). And the equity (the total cash investments upfront) would be a little over $1.625 million ($4.875 million less debt of $3.25 million). Equity investors, in total, could have a $975,002 combined year-one tax write-off on a $1.625 million investment. This gives investors a 60 percent of investment tax write-off in year one alone.

Passive investors are limited on their usage of this benefit and may have to carry forward a portion of their losses. But qualified real estate professionals (QREPs) may be able to use all of their losses against both active and passive income in that first year. More on QREPs later.

Nothing is perfect. Take note that the taxable income will be higher in later years, after the impact of accelerated depreciation ends. And also note that taxes will be due for depreciation recapture upon the sale of the asset unless you swap the property for another through a 1031 tax deferred exchange. And that is the subject of our next tax savings tip.

Defer Taxes Through a 1031 Exchange

We almost lost our beloved 1031 exchange in the 2017 tax reform bill. Speculation swirled about the end of this benefit for months that fall. When the news broke in late December, investors in numerous asset classes were deeply disappointed. Art, vehicles, airplanes, and other investments would no longer be swappable. But real estate survived unscathed.

A 1031 exchange is a swap of one investment property for another that allows capital gains and depreciation recapture taxes to be deferred. The swap does not have to be a direct A for B exchange, and, in fact, I've never heard of a swap that followed that script.

A typical 1031 exchange involves the sale of one property (the "relinquished property") with all proceeds held by a qualified intermediary. Within 45 days, the seller of the relinquished property selects up to three (sometimes more) potential replacement properties that may be acquired with the funds. The selected property/properties must close within 180 days total from the time of the original sale.

All of the capital gains taxes and previously unpaid taxes saved through depreciation (depreciation recapture) will be deferred to the sale of the next property. Deferrals may continue through another 1031 exchange later.

The 1031 exchange has a number of potential benefits. First of all, the math on growing a portfolio through tax deferred reinvestments clearly results in a higher portfolio value. Second, some investors choose to consolidate a number of small properties (like residential homes) into a larger property (like a commercial self-storage asset). Management of a large property can be easier than managing a number of small properties. Third, the depreciation schedule is reset to day one, which means the accelerated depreciation benefits can start over again with the replacement property. Fourth, some investors use a 1031 exchange to replace a non cash flowing asset (like land) with a cash flowing asset (like a self-storage facility). Lastly, some investors use a 1031 exchange as part of a relocation from a state they want to get out of and into a property located where they want to move or retire.

There are a number of disadvantages that must be navigated as part of a 1031 exchange. One is the fact that regulations and timelines must be strictly followed. An exchange may be disallowed if not followed to the letter. Secondly, the tight timeline can cause a lot of stress and a loss of negotiating power. When sellers get wind that this is an exchange, they may refuse to negotiate when problems arise in the process (because they know the buyer has limited options). These issues result in the abandonment of many exchanges in-process. Thirdly, the replacement property must cost more than the combined equity and debt from the relinquished property. Taxes on the difference (called "boot") may result otherwise. Lastly, some argue that future tax hikes may override the benefit of savings from deferred in early years. I would argue that the time value of money will outweigh this, but I may eventually be proven wrong.

The difficulty in finding suitable replacement properties and the egregious timelines have caused many to criticize or abandon the 1031 exchange opportunity. I was wary of it myself at some points—especially during the decade-plus post Great Financial Crisis runup in real estate prices. Recently, I've found three tactics that can sometimes bail out a 1031 in crisis. Investors who want to defer taxes through an exchange but don't want the hassle of finding and managing a replacement property can consider these potential scenarios.

1. **Delaware Statutory Trust**: A DST is an ownership model that creates a legal entity allowing co-investment among sponsors and accredited investors to purchase fractional beneficial interests in either a single asset or a portfolio of properties. DSTs are tax-deferred and 1031 exchange-friendly. This structure has a variety of benefits including tax deferral, offloading of management responsibilities to a pro, the opportunity to buy a small or large portion of the asset, the assumption of all debt by the operator (none by the investor), diversification, and the elimination of the pressure caused by timelines. This is my favorite of the three alternative 1031 strategies.

2. **Monetized Installment Sale:** This is a strategy that inserts a third party between the seller and the buyer to allow the seller to treat the sale as an installment sale (essentially owner financing over time).

This defers the tax until the sale is finalized (typically in two to three decades) but allows the seller to access the majority (typically up to about 95 percent) of the proceeds immediately through a loan.

3. **Deferred Sales Trust**: This strategy allows a trust to acquire the seller's property and sell it to the ultimate buyer. The seller treats the transaction as a "seller-carryback" where the buyer (the trust in this case) pays for the purchase over time. The proceeds are invested in income-producing assets along the way for the benefit of the seller.

The benefits of the 1031 exchange are wonderful, but everyone has to pay the piper someday. *Unless they don't.* Many investors who have done multiple 1031 exchanges have found that this next strategy is the crown jewel of all and will extend tax deferrals into the next life. Well, sort of.

My dad told me there are two things you can't avoid in this life: death and taxes. I've found that some people dread the latter more than the former. Well, you'll be glad to know that this strategy can potentially avoid the tax part at least. You'll have to figure out the other part on your own.

My friend Lambert bought a property in the 1970s. It had appreciated handsomely when he went to sell it in the early 1990s, and he dreaded paying taxes on the capital gains and the depreciation recapture. He learned about the new 1031 exchange regulations, and he was all-in. When it came time to sell that property years later, he did another 1031 exchange. And then another later.

When he hit 70, he knew he didn't want to be a landlord in his golden years. He was ready to sell the last property in the chain and take the tax hit. Then he sat down with his CPA and did the numbers. He was devastated. The accumulated taxes would wipe out a significant portion of what he had built up over many decades. But Lambert's astute CPA informed him that if he was still holding an exchanged property at the time of his (and his wife's) passing, then his heirs would get a step-up in basis. This means the value of the property would be reset to the time of death and the capital gains and recapture taxes would be zeroed out.

With renewed vigor, Lambert set out to find a replacement property and do (at least) one more 1031 exchange. He was determined to kick the can down the road before he kicked the bucket. Lambert actually discovered the Delaware Statutory Trust vehicle, and happily invested in one as his replacement property.

By deferring taxes again, and planning to continue this until death, his heirs will theoretically owe no gain and recapture taxes on at least five (or up to seven) decades of gains. This is a great start to being remembered favorably by your heirs, wouldn't you agree?

My 1031 qualified intermediary told me the story of the swap till you drop strategy being used over three generations and counting. An older man and wife passed a commercial property along to their adult child at their death in the 90s. There was a step-up in basis and no taxes were owed. The adult child performed a few 1031 exchanges in the next 25 years before he passed away, leaving another step-up in basis and another zero-tax bill. The grandchildren are now enjoying profits from this property that has grown in value with no capital gain or depreciation recapture taxes. Maybe you'll start a similar multigenerational tax saving legacy! I hope to.

Correctly Classify Deductible Repairs

Starting today I hope you won't allow a CPA with a tax-prep only mentality determine your tax strategy. Also, don't let an uninformed clerk decide which of your business expenses are capitalized and which are fully deductible in the current year. Capitalized expenses are typically depreciated over several (often 5 to 39) years. But this is unnecessary for so many expenses.

Repairs to the property don't usually need to be capitalized and depreciated. They can typically be absorbed as an expense in the current year. For example, if you replace your 25-year-old roof with a new one, it is likely depreciable over a number of years. But if your current roof is damaged and a section is replaced, this repair may be able to be treated as an expense in the current year. These items can add up. Speaking of fully deducting expenses in the current year...

Section 179 Deductible Expenses

Section 179 of the Internal Revenue Code allows operators to fully deduct certain investments in their business that may otherwise be classified as capital expenses (which are depreciated over time). The Tax Cuts and Jobs Act of 2017 expanded the limit of these items to $1 million.

Items that may be deducted under Section 179 include HVAC; fire suppression; security and alarm systems; roofing; business equipment; business vehicles weighing over 6,000 pounds; computers and off-the-shelf software; office furniture and equipment; and certain non-structural components of commercial buildings (e.g., a printing press).

Self-Directed Retirement Fund Options

Have you had a corporate 401(k) or pension plan? I had three in years past, and I always wished I had more investment options within them. Almost 20 years ago, I learned that I could invest in real estate using my retirement funds. I set up two individual retirement accounts (IRAs), and I have never looked back.

There are two major categories of IRAs: The simplified employee pension (SEP IRA) and the Roth IRA. Both of these plans may be self-directed, which means investors have a lot of freedom to invest where they wish. There are certain limitations, however, and I would caution investors not to speculate with their freedom.

The SEP IRA provides business owners with a simple method to contribute to their employees' as well as their own retirement plans. Many self-employed investors set these up just for themselves. The contributions made to these plans are tax deductible, meaning they are a cost of doing business to the employer and therefore considered pre-tax funds. The principal and growth in these funds will be taxed later, at a presumably lower post-retirement tax rate.

The Roth IRA is a retirement savings account that uses after-tax contributions. The investments in a Roth IRA grow tax-free, and withdrawals are not taxed either. This plan was established in 1997 and is named after Senator Roth from Delaware. It has been called one of the worst mistakes made by Congress (because of lower revenues to the government). In that sense, it may be one of the best opportunities for you to grow wealth.

An additional option for some self-employed individuals is a self-directed solo 401(k) plan. You can't use this plan if you have any full-time employees, but you can cover you and your spouse. The solo 401(k) has higher contribution limits than IRAs but a number of restrictions as well. A percentage of contributions from actively generated income can be used for contributions, which will likely lower total tax but increase FICA (Social Security and Medicare) taxes for some people.

Investor, beware! Before I understood the difference between investing and speculating, as I discuss in the next chapter, I made a number of mistakes in my IRA investments. I caution you to treat these funds with great care and to invest them just as you would any other cash you have on-hand.

Avoid Passive Loss Limitations as a QREP

Passive investors in a real estate investment can deduct a limited amount of passive losses (like losses from depreciation) from their income. This amount can be carried forward, but it will always be limited to shield passive (not active) gains. Active real estate investors cannot shield earned (active) income with passive losses. Only passive gains can be shielded with passive losses.

There are two exceptions. First, if your modified adjusted gross income (MAGI) is up to $100,000, you can deduct up to $25,000 of passive losses against other income. From $100,000–$150,000, this allowance is phased out. The second exception is to become a qualified real estate professional (QREP). In general, a QREP can deduct unlimited passive losses against active and passive income. This could dramatically alter your tax situation.

There are many hurdles to qualify as a QREP, but here are a few major ones. First, over half of the personal services performed by the individual must be performed in the real estate realm. Second, the taxpayer must spend over 750 hours per year in real estate activities. Additionally, the individual must prove they were material participants in these real estate activities. There are seven tests to provide evidence of this and not every test must be passed to qualify. (For example, one test asks if investors participate in real estate activities on a "regular, continuous, and substantial basis during the year.") Also note that some investors who become a QREP but can't meet these qualifications have spouses who can, so doing that and then filing jointly could solve the problem. Of course talk with your CPA or tax strategist before making big decisions.

Climbing the Ladder of Self-Storage Success

A lot of real estate investors plot a course to climb the ladder in residential or multifamily investing. For many, this is a process of acquiring a rental home, fixing it up, leasing it out, and selling it. With the profits they acquire, say, a duplex and repeat the process. Then they use those profits to acquire a fourplex and work their way up from there.

I wondered whether this could be done in self-storage as well. The answer is: yes it can. My friend AJ Osborne (check out his *BiggerPockets Real Estate Podcast* interviews in Episodes 286 and 388) acquired a small 17,000-square-foot self-storage facility late in the Great Recession for $260,000. He made quite a few improvements, increased the income, and sold it sometime later for $620,000. He used the proceeds plus new debt to acquire a 36,000-square-foot facility for $1.4 million. He improved it, increased the income, and sold it just 18 months later for $2.2 million. Netting $950,000 in this transaction and implementing a 1031 tax-deferred exchange became his basis to acquire a 70,000-square-foot facility for $4 million. He added just $100,000 in upgrades, so he had $1,050,000 in cash in this project plus debt. After upgrading, improving income, and expanding the facility, he doubled its value.

Though it took a great deal of work along the way, his initial investment of under $100,000 cash plus $100,000 in additional cash later resulted in ownership of a profitable $8 million asset. And it has generated years of income along the way. Because he is a direct owner, is a QREP, implemented cost segregation, and utilized a 1031 exchange, he has paid very little in taxes throughout this process.

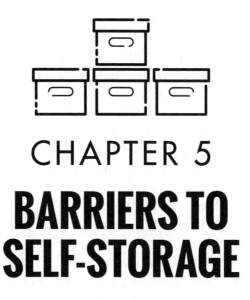

CHAPTER 5

BARRIERS TO SELF-STORAGE

It's really no secret. The super-wealthy perpetuate their fortunes by investing in assets the average investor has no practical access to. As we've already discussed, many of the Forbes 400 made their fortunes through commercial real estate. So, what holds most of us back?

Even a cursory review of the commercial real estate realm reveals that the majority of us cannot get meaningful direct access to this profitable investment class, especially in a way that doesn't come with the burden of crushing debt and massive time commitment. And if you don't know what you're doing, you could get burned.

Why You're *Not* Invited to Their Party

When I was in business school, we learned about the importance of erecting strategic barriers to entry around our products or companies. How could we ensure that competitors were blocked from entering our space?

Some rely on patents, some on controlling a scarce resource. High setup or research and development costs can keep others out, along with predatory pricing, brand loyalty, and vertical integration. Barriers to entry are obviously great for those who erect them, and frustrating to those on the outside.

The barriers to entry in commercial investing are significant. You cannot easily enter this space. This is not an easy path to wealth. What are some of these barriers to entry, and why is it so hard?

Before I go on, I want to let you know that some of the information I'm about to share may sound discouraging. Don't despair! Section III of this book is designed to show you seven paths to enter the self-storage business. Many of these paths allow you to circumvent some of the requirements I'm explaining here. You have options!

Barrier 1: Cash Requirements

How big is your piggy bank? The cash required for projects of profitable scale is high.

Have you seen those "make a fortune in real estate with no money down" infomercials? I guess that's possible, but I've been deeply entrenched in many aspects of real estate for two decades, and I've only seen a few commercial deals like that. Though they may exist somewhere, low- or no-money-down deals aren't common in the realm of safe, profitable, repeatable commercial real estate investing.

We'll talk about safe, profitable scale in a moment. Suffice it to say that the scale is in the 30,000-square-foot-plus range, and properties like that typically cost in the millions, generally over $5 million. But let's say you want to start smaller, such as with a $1 million facility. You will need to put about 25 to 30 percent down, or at least $250,000. You will also need cash to make lender-mandated repairs, implement improvements to increase rents, and maintain mortgage payment and repair reserves.

Therefore, you should consider about $300,000 cash or more as a good starting point (in this example at least). Since the risk-return law is often linked to the law of diversification, this allocation should be only a part of your portfolio. Hopefully you've got something like a million dollars (or more) to get in. (In a moment, I'll give you a second reason this figure is a good minimum.) Some of you might have this available or have access to funds like this through your network. But unless you're paying cash, that still won't get you through the door. You need to qualify for debt financing.

Barrier 2: Loan Qualifications

Self-storage experience required. This is a quandary for aspiring investors. You may reason that you need to start small and build up in order to gain experience. This is certainly one option, and I will explain that path (Path 1) in section III. Seriously, in order to qualify for debt financing, it will be best for you to have credible experience (or have access to others' expertise) for at least three reasons:

1. The lender looks carefully at your experience and the experience of your team. It's not like buying your first home. Banks have this thing for wanting to get their money back, and experience is a big indicator.

2. The broker and seller may scrutinize you. Again, unlike residential realtors, commercial realtors do not have to present every offer to the sellers. They will only give the time of day to those who they believe are serious. They will not bother with someone they think can't close and could ruin the sale for their seller and them (more on this soon).

3. You will need this experience (or have access to it through expert advice) to successfully operate the property.

In addition to requiring significant self-storage experience, lenders will want to see a significant personal balance sheet. Even non-recourse lenders will typically require personal assets equal to the balance of the loan. Non-recourse debt means that the lender will not come after your personal assets—except in rare cases—if the debt is in default.

Did you catch that? In addition to the value of the asset you're purchasing, lenders will want to see other assets totaling at least the value of the loan you are applying for. This can be from you or others who sign for the loan.

In the $1 million/75 percent LTV example, this means the buyer must come up with about $300,000 or so in cash to put down and make repairs, etc. And they will need significant other liquid assets (perhaps a million dollars) for debt service required by the lender. This is not to mention a clear track record, a great credit score, no bankruptcies or short sales, etc. This is not a set formula, and it varies by situation and lender, but trust me when I say that this is a significant barrier for most investors.

Barrier 3: Commercial Brokers

It's all about who you know. As I said, in contrast to residential realtors, commercial brokers are not required to present all offers to their sellers, and they don't. Brokers typically work with a small pool of experienced buyers whom they know will be able to close deals.

I helped my business partner build a beautiful Hyatt House hotel in the Midwest some years ago. After studying the powerful market fundamentals in Texas, we decided Houston would be our next target city. I spent some time on the ground there, and after studying a variety of land parcels, we wrote up an LOI to buy a certain commercial parcel near the heart of the booming Texas Medical Center.

We offered nearly full price (about $7 million for an acre) and submitted it to the owner through his broker. Days went by, then more than a week. We were surprised he hadn't accepted or countered our offer right away. When I finally got the broker on the phone, it became fairly obvious that he hadn't even presented it to the seller, or at least the seller had paid it little mind. I was flabbergasted. Didn't he know who we were?

That's exactly the point. He had no idea who we were, and he was too busy to find out. In his mind, we didn't seem like people who would put food on his table or gas in his BMW, so we were initially ignored. To this broker, I was a random caller—a dreamer hoping to buy an expensive property. My lingo, comments, and questions gave me away. I was an amateur.

Okay, it's not just about who you know; it's also about what you've done. As with lenders, commercial brokers want to see experience, other assets owned and operated, and a positive track record from offer to close and beyond. They will ask for references and pointedly inquire about how many other accepted offers you closed or failed to close on and why. They will ask you where your equity is coming from and how you know you can qualify for debt, and even request details on your financial projections for the property.

One client, or even one large deal, may provide the majority of the broker's annual income, and they refuse to take any risks dealing with unknown buyers. The risks of not closing mean they will have egg on their face and have to go back to the buyer pool to seek a new offer. This will raise concerns about the property and could easily result in a lower price.

Even if the buyer is positioned to close, the broker will want to ensure that this buyer won't significantly "retrade" on the way to closing. This can result when an uninformed buyer gets bad news during inspections and tries to renegotiate with the seller, or they just try to save money by renegotiating. This can be frustrating and costly for the broker and the seller, and they want to avoid buyers with a reputation for doing this.

Brokers will often advise their sellers to take a lower offer from a known buyer, thus, heightening this barrier for those not in their inner circle. Like other barriers, it's possible to overcome, but it's by no means easy.

Barrier 4: Economies of Scale

Go big or go home. I was involved in multifamily before self-storage, and when I first started to see the demographic trends that drive the multi-family sector, I immediately considered purchasing a six-unit apartment building in a nice part of town. It wasn't on the market, it was fully leased, and no big problems surfaced in my cursory reviews. I talked to the owner personally. "This seems profitable to you. Why are you selling?"

"Well, I'm just tired. Tired of screening tenants, tired of Saturday calls, tired of trying to be a mom and a property manager. I'm trying to start a new medical business, and I can't do everything. But you could probably pull it off since you've been in real estate a long time."

That's a pretty standard answer among sellers of small properties. Yes, many get an off-site property manager, and that can work. But the cost per unit to run a small complex is much greater than a large one. A large complex can afford on-site staff, and that's one way economies of scale really kicks in.

Many self-storage operators see this economy starting at about 300 to 400 units or about 30,000 to 40,000 square feet. Economies of scale at 500 are certainly better than at 300. For example, the property manager's salary on a 500-unit complex isn't much higher than that of the 300-unit manager. The marketing on a 500-unit property may be similar to that on a 300-unit property as well. There are many other ways the scale works in favor of the large property owner, which is effectively another barrier to a new investor in this space.

Large properties also have access to multiple streams of income that are unavailable to the small owner. For example, large properties (particularly portfolios) can set up a cooperative insurance policy for renters' insurance. New renters add $10 or so per month to their rent to buy their insurance, but up to $5 of that comes back to the property owner if claims are low. This can really add up and increase property value. Large properties may also be better suited to higher truck rental revenues, which can be quite substantial as well.

A 500-unit property where 65 percent of the renters buy in-house renters' insurance ($5 per month revenue) will increase their revenue by $19,500 annually. At a 6.5 percent cap rate, this simple item translates to an increase in asset value of over $300,000. This is equity in the owner's pocket at the time of refinance or sale. Hopefully this reminds you of the power of professionally owned commercial real estate. And I hope it encourages you to skip over the small properties and figure out how to go big.

Barrier 5: REIT Conspiracy

As in any other business, a smart operator will be competing against others in their market. Institutional players have the resources, time, technology, and smarts to win, so be careful about picking a fight with them.

- They can beat you on **price**. (They don't have to make a profit every quarter.)
- They can beat you on **marketing**.
- They can often beat you on **aesthetics**.
- They beat most on **location**.
- They can beat you on **technology**.

The conspiracy thing can actually come into play like this: In some cases, institutional players may not only want to beat you; they may want to acquire you. It's said that these smart operators will do what they can to drive you to a place of low income, which is a double whammy to a commercial real estate operator. It can drive you to a place where you need to sell, and it can lower your value so much that you'll have to sell cheaply (remember our value formula: **Value = NOI / Cap Rate**).

What's the solution to this barrier? Here are a few thoughts:

- Be careful about your location. (We discuss this in chapters 6 and 7.)
- Commit to be a great operator with an invaluable staff.
- Out-market them on the ground. (There are many ways to do this. A committed salesperson/manager who gets out in the community can create opportunities that can beat a corporate program.)
- Adopt effective cutting-edge technology for marketing and operations.

Unlike many businesses, this is not one you can easily tiptoe into part time. And that's just the way the insiders want to keep it.

How *do* you get access? I didn't write this book just to frustrate you. There are meaningful ways to access the historic returns, principal safety, and surprising tax avoidance enjoyed by commercial self-storage property owners.

Section III of this volume outlines seven different paths you can follow to attain success in commercial-level self-storage investing. I'm excited to share these paths with you, and I'm certain you will find one or more that is a great fit for you.

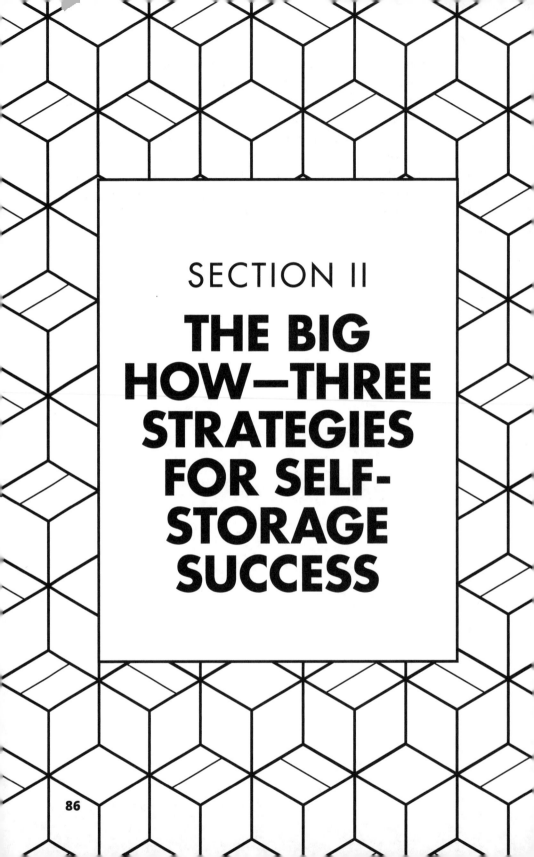

SECTION II

THE BIG HOW—THREE STRATEGIES FOR SELF-STORAGE SUCCESS

CHAPTER 6

SUCCESS STRATEGY 1: GROUND-UP DEVELOPMENT

By now, I hope you're convinced that self-storage is a viable, profitable, and potentially wonderful asset class that deserves your time, focus, and funding.

Perhaps you're wondering, "How does this work? You've given me many reasons why I *should* love self-storage investing. You've laid out lots of details on how to grow revenue and value. But I need to *understand* the details. What are the most successful strategies used by self-storage syndicator/operators?" I'm so glad you asked. We'll start with the first strategy to building self-storage success.

Ground-up development is the riskiest—and potentially most rewarding—of the three major strategies. As I discussed earlier, low risk typically leads to low return, and higher risk typically leads to higher *potential* return. But it can also produce the highest potential loss.

12 Major Steps

This strategy involves developing a new self-storage facility where there is none now. Ground-up development involves at least 12 major steps, or functions. All are critically important.

1. Location identification
2. Feasibility study
3. Survey/site plan/environmental studies
4. Land acquisition
5. Entitlements
6. Design
7. Lender approval
8. Investor interface
9. Contractor selection
10. Project oversight/management
11. Property manager selection
12. Asset management

Location Identification

The first step in the process is identifying a good location. Initially, this could be an underserved region, a city, a submarket, a neighborhood, or even an exact location.

Would-be developers stumble upon a prospective location in a wide variety of ways. Some own a piece of land already. Others are offered a parcel. Others are intentionally looking in an area in which they wish to build. As I've mentioned elsewhere, you will want to examine:

- **Density**: We're talking density of storage versus population in the area. (The goal is under about seven square feet of storage per person in a three- to five-mile radius, though other issues like population density, region, etc. should be taken into consideration.)
- **Traffic Count**: You should expect 10,000 or more vehicles per day to drive by in a low-population density area, or hopefully 30,000 or more vehicles per day in a more densely populated region.
- **Visibility**: It's not enough to be on a well-traveled road; you must have high visibility, not be hidden behind a hill or a Walmart.
- **Signage Opportunity**: You want to have frontage that will allow for ingress, egress, and great signage.
- **Income**: You don't need to be in a wealthy neighborhood (though it is a plus), but we like to see income above the national and local average.

Feasibility Study

Don't skimp on this. If you are planning to invest years of your life and millions of dollars in a project, spend the money to get an independent feasibility study on the project and the location. This may come later in the timeline, but it needs to happen—with many bankers requiring it. The study will include:

- **Subject Location Inspection**: This includes maps, photos, descriptions, survey, site attributes, and more.
- **Market Review**: This includes demographics, neighborhood, competitor locations, competitor analysis, demand analysis, market inventory, unit mix and rates, pricing volatility, regional trends, national trends, and more.
- **Lease-Up Period**: This "absorption" analysis will be critical for your project.
- **Financial Analysis**: This includes income statements and more.
- **Operations/Marketing/Development Recommendations**: The expert conducting the study has broad experience that allows them to provide helpful advice on strategies to increase income and reduce costs.
- **General Information about Self-Storage**: This includes general information on zoning, the life cycle, development costs and time frame, financing, expenses, valuation methodology, and more.
- **Conclusions and Recommendations**: The study will provide advice that will help prospective operators make a decision on whether to move forward or not.

Survey/Site Plan/Environmental Studies

A lot of work goes into the process of acquiring a parcel of commercial land. At some point in the process, the seller, buyer, and broker will work together to produce a significant amount of documentation like this and more.

- **Survey**: Using the deed description, former surveys, and on-the-ground measurements, a surveyor will produce an official drawing of the boundary, significant structures, and more.
- **Site Plan**: This is a set of construction drawings used by an owner or contractor to make improvements to a property and to allow enforcement officials to verify code is being followed.
- **Environmental Studies**: This documents prior environmental hazards as well as potential impacts from future projects.

Land Acquisition

The process of acquiring the land typically goes through several stages. This is much more involved than acquiring land for residential use.

- **Letter of intent (LOI)**: Typically, a developer first ties up a parcel of land through a letter of intent. This LOI is converted to a contract with the help of brokers and attorneys.
- **Deposit**: As part of the contract, the purchaser typically puts down refundable and/or nonrefundable earnest money, which gives them the exclusive right to perform due diligence for a certain period of time (typically many months or even more than a year).
- **Due diligence**: The purchaser's due diligence (in conjunction with the seller) will include site survey, environmental studies, feasibility study, meetings with municipalities, zoning confirmation or variance, and sometimes even building permits.
- **Hard earnest money**: After certain hurdles are crossed or time limits have been reached, the purchaser typically confirms that a certain portion of the earnest money goes *hard*, or nonrefundable.
- **Closing**: Eventually all contingencies are met (or some are waived) and the closing takes place.

Entitlements

There are a variety of hoops that a developer must jump through with the city, township, or county. Some of these are simple matters of filed paperwork and a nominal fee. Others may result in a costly battle. One of the risks for developers is doing all this work before even owning the property. One non-approval late in the game can bring the whole project to a screeching halt. And it can potentially gobble up a boatload of the developer's capital and time.

This preapproval "at-risk" capital is costlier due to the greater risk of loss. Whether tendered by the developer or a third party, the ensuing interest rate or ownership stake is more valuable than investments tendered later in the process, after there is more certainty.

The entitlement process can be lengthy and frustrating, not only because of dealing with bureaucrats but also due to possible neighborhood opposition, which can be illogical.

An associate of mine flew from California to Nashville, Tennessee, almost a dozen times for meetings with a municipality, architects, engineers, homeowner associations, and a neighboring school to get a property entitled for self-storage. They got the land inexpensively because the prior owner had failed in the same process. A difficult entitling process can be a big advantage to developers, however. If it's that hard, hopefully it will keep competition out.

Our Wellings Growth Fund recently invested in a self-storage development in the Minneapolis, Minnesota, area. The city was not excited about self-storage in residential areas, and, in fact, they had rezoned to permit self-storage in industrial parks only. Fortunately, this property had been entitled by the previous owner before that change. This, along with the significant lack of competitors in the growing residential area, gave us great encouragement to invest.

Design

Like many of the previously mentioned items, design is difficult to place on a strict timeline. Some developers know what they want to build before they find a location. Others design around the location, which may relate to the region or the site topography. Still others create a design under the mandate of the municipality. Some design according to a corporate/ franchise style mandate.

The Nashville developer created a beautiful design based on the horse stable motif that is popular in that area. Other designs are based on brand continuity within a franchise. I know of a location on a hillside that was designed with drive-up storage bays on two levels (front and back, like a walkout basement).

Some storage facility designs were changed from steel siding to HardiePlank or brick to meet local zoning requirements. I know of one case where zoning didn't require brick, but the developer was forced to do a brick facade as a condition of the city's approval.

The design process may include architects, soil engineers, structural engineers, estimators, and more. It is possible to get a preliminary design in order to obtain initial approvals, close on the land, and then undertake a final design to receive building permits.

The cost of design is another expense that is sometimes fully or partially borne by the developer or early investors before they know the project is approved. It's another risk that could sink a developer—or make them wealthy.

Lender Approval

If you're using debt as part of your project, you will be working with a lender. As I discuss in chapter 5, this is often not a slam dunk. Lenders want your business, but they have fences designed to keep newbies and bad players out.

Terry Campbell of Live Oak Bank is one of the nation's most aggressive self-storage lenders. Although the bank is only a dozen years old, it has become one of the major Small Business Association lenders in the United States. According to Terry, there are five Cs to being *lendable*. These are characteristics bankers look at when deciding whether to lend to you:

1. **Character**—personal and business reputation of the borrower (includes credit score)
2. **Capacity**—ability to repay the loan
3. **Capital**—borrower's investment and reserves
4. **Collateral**—receivables, equipment, and other assets that act as security for the loan
5. **Conditions**—state of the national and local economy, industry outlook, project's competitive position, etc.

You will have to work with the bank to decide whether you want a convertible long-term loan or just a construction/bridge loan for your project. There are advantages to each, depending on factors that include your ownership horizon, desire to refinance, and the lender's preferences, among other things. (I'm oversimplifying for the sake of brevity.) This is something that you want to be sure you have lined up before going too far down the development road.

Investor Interface

If you're planning to include equity investors, you will obviously need to develop relationships with them long before you start this process. It's not true that money automatically flows straight to great projects. There is a lot more involved, and much of it has to do with the developer. There are so many things that need to be done right, but here are a few things *not* to do:

- Don't assume everyone else will be as optimistic as you are.
- Don't rely on a single large investor (unless it's you, and even that should be suspect).

- Don't expect to get a large institutional or wealthy backer.
- Don't count on a large check from China or India.
- Don't expect to get crowdfunding (no matter what've you heard).

That may sound pretty pessimistic, but I have made many of these mistakes myself, and I know others who have as well. This is the big leagues, and you need to figure this out before you move to square one.

Contractor Selection

Are you a seasoned commercial general contractor? If so, you may not need to select a contractor. Otherwise, you will need to hire a general contractor to manage your project. Though building self-storage is less involved than many other commercial construction types, it's never a cakewalk. And the penalties for mistakes can be deadly.

Please, do not automatically go with the lowest bidder. Vet several contractors first. Otherwise, that low bid may wind up costing you much more if you have to fire the contractor, redo the work, or even pay the subcontractors after the contractor has taken off with the money.

Often the lowest bidder:
- plans to substitute low-quality materials or take other shortcuts;
- is inexperienced and doesn't know what they don't know;
- is underinsured or uninsured;
- didn't include something important in the bid and doesn't plan to inform you of that until you're way down the road ("That'll be another change order.");
- plans to do the work themselves to cut corners; or
- is unpopular, needs the work, and therefore underbids.

Project Oversight/Management

If you're the developer, you must stay deeply involved as the project manager. Regardless of how good the general contractor is, the lender, investors, and municipality are counting on *you* to ensure that the facility is built right, on time, and within budget.

This can consume months or even a year or more of your life, so make sure you count the cost before you go down this road. And make sure you have a great team in place to help you along the way.

Property Manager Selection

Who will manage your property once it is open? Get them involved early on, so they can begin to develop a business plan during the initial phases of construction. Start looking for the key employee who will run your multimillion-dollar facility.

Unless you've already got an experienced team in place, I recommend contracting with a significant national property management firm. If your facility is too small to get its attention, you may consider implementing automated options (kiosks, etc.) or finding a local live-in manager. There are many great national and regional property management firms, and some are part of REITs. Choose wisely. And again, don't assume that the lowest bidder is the best option.

Asset Management

Once you are up and running, that's no signal to relax. Though things will certainly slow down, you will still be responsible for overseeing the property manager, providing a budget, watching the numbers, providing financial reports to lenders, providing reports to investors, processing investor distributions, making regular property visits, and much more. This is your property, and the buck stops with you.

The property manager may have many ideas about marketing the property, but what to do and how much to spend will be your decision. The property manager may give you many reasons why lease-up is slower than expected, but you will have to determine whether the reasons are valid. If competitor pricing is below normal, it's you who will have to decide to keep your prices higher or follow suit. It might be the property manager who misses the annual tax payment, but the municipality will look to you to pay the fine.

Even if the investors understand that the economy is softening, that natural disaster is once in a lifetime, or U-Haul's brakes are the company's responsibility, they will be looking to you to provide answers for their lower-than-expected distribution checks.

This is true under any of the strategies addressed in this section, of course. Unless you are a merchant developer, you will be tasked as the asset manager or you'll pay someone to fulfill this role. And you know that no one cares as much as the owner and others with significant skin in the game. Speaking of merchant developers...

Build-To-Operate Versus Merchant Developers

Before ending this chapter, I want to clearly delineate two potential and vastly different paths within this ground-up development model. They start the same but end up completely different.

Everything I've covered in this chapter is about the build-to-operate model. It assumes that you are building the self-storage facility to operate it during the lease-up period and likely beyond. You (or the syndicator you invest with) are building this facility to generate cash flow for yourself and your investors for years to come.

Of course, this doesn't mean that you wouldn't consider an offer to sell at a great price at some point after construction. A smart developer will build a facility that can be held or sold. Nearly everything is for sale at some price, right?

Some developers build self-storage facilities with the intent to sell them at the completion of construction (at CO—certificate of occupancy) or during lease-up. Also known as merchant builders, these developers are in the business of making money from development. They are happy to collect their profits sooner rather than later and reinvest them in the next project. They like to build, but they prefer not to operate. This could be a great strategy for you as a potential syndicator or investor.

In the event that the facilities don't sell when expected, the smart merchant developer is typically okay with refinancing out of their construction loan and holding the asset long term to operate and profit from. The economy/investors' desires may have changed, the lending environment may be different, or the project may have turned out better (or worse) than expected.

Since both scenarios could be reversed (the build-to-operate developer may sell, and the merchant developer could hold), I highly recommend that you build financial models up front that consider both scenarios. This will be best for you, your lenders, and your investors.

A Ground-Up Development Example

I mentioned that we invested in a ground-up self-storage development in Ramsey, Minnesota, near Minneapolis. The total cost of the project is around $10 million, consisting of about $7 million in debt plus about $3 million in investor equity. The independent due diligence report on this facility projects a value at stabilization of over $17 million. There are at least four scenarios that could play out with the project, and all four are great for us.

1. We could sell the project to an institutional investor (like a REIT or life insurance company) at Certificate of Occupancy. This would be in approximately 14 months, and we project that the sales price would be at least $13 million. Since there is a total equity investment of under $3 million, this could approximately double our money (from $3 million to $6 million) in a little over a year. That's a 100 percent total annual return. Downside: We would have to figure out where to reinvest our capital, a problem I'd be happy to solve.

2. We could sell the asset at stabilization. This would be approximately two or more years after the completion of construction. If we were able to sell the asset at that time for, say, $15 million to $17 million, we would hope to generate an annual return of about 40 percent or more to investors. This is certainly possible.

3. We could sell the asset in about six years. This would be at a point of very predictable income. Investors would benefit from three or so years of ongoing distributions plus the sale of the facility for (theoretically) top dollar. We have projected annual net returns to investors of about 28 percent in this scenario.

4. We could refinance the asset, returning investors' principal, and continue to operate the asset medium or long term. This would effectively provide investors with a tax-free return of their principal, which would allow them to reinvest somewhere else. This is a way to generate two trees of income from one seed. The refinance could happen in as little as three years, at stabilization. Investor returns could be delayed a bit and would be partially dependent on the second investment. But total returns would likely be ultimately higher than in many other scenarios, especially if this scenario is repeated again and again.

Imagine starting with one investment and seeing your portfolio effectively doubling every three to five years. It would be hard to pull off with many risks and challenges along the way, but it has been done. Maybe you'll be the next one to make it happen!

CHAPTER 7

SUCCESS STRATEGY 2: VALUE-ADD SELF-STORAGE

This is my favorite self-storage success strategy, and the one our funds are investing in most heavily.

From Mom-and-Pop to Stabilized Operation to REIT

Recall that one of the truly favorable aspects of the self-storage business is the fragmentation of ownership. The fragmented nature of the current ownership in U.S. self-storage facilities provides an unparalleled (in my experience) opportunity to buy an underperforming facility and upgrade it. The result could be an opportunity to flip it to an institutional buyer at a lower cap rate (higher price) or to hold it to provide enhanced cash flow for years to come.

Fragmentation Review

As a reminder, here's what I mean by a fragmented ownership situation.

As of this writing, there are nearly 50,000 self-storage facilities in the United States. Only about 28 percent of these facilities are owned and operated by REITs and other large players, meaning that about 72 percent are operated by small operators, including mom-and-pops.[22] This means there could be tens of thousands of U.S. self-storage facilities that are undermanaged, underperforming, undermarketed, and below their potential value.

At the same time, commercial real estate investing has risen to new heights of popularity. At the time of this writing, multifamily prices have risen to dizzying, unprecedented heights. There is more money, from inside the United States and abroad, chasing commercial real estate deals than ever before.

A lot of syndicators and investors are pushing pause on their pursuit of multifamily and some other popular commercial real estate asset classes. This includes single-family rentals and small multifamily properties, which are also overpriced at the moment. Many are turning to alternative assets like self-storage.

What's happening at this individual level is also happening on a larger scale among institutional investors like REITs, private equity funds, life insurance companies, large self-storage operators, exchange buyers, and other large investors. They have funds that need to be invested to make a return. They are looking for alternatives in an overheated market.

QUICK INSIGHTS

Competition

It used to be that small multifamily and other commercial investors didn't often compete with institutional investors for deals. REITs and others focused on gateway or primary cities; looked for large, stabilized deals; and acquired newer, Class A assets.

Due to the intense competition for return, these investors are now competing for smaller deals in smaller cities. They're tolerating less-stabilized, older, and smaller deals. Generally, they're coming from coastal cities into the heartland of America trying to find yield. They were already used to accepting lower returns for the sake of predictability; now they are going even lower.

---

22 *2020 Self-Storage Almanac*

This has made it hard for multifamily and other commercial investors to compete. It has driven investors of all types to accept lower returns and seek alternative assets.

What has happened in multifamily is already happening in self-storage and other asset classes. This competition is trickling down to smaller assets in less-desirable locations, which is putting the squeeze on ground-up development as well as cash-flowing stabilized facilities. This creates a greater need than ever before for strategic creativity. The value-add strategy in this chapter and the retrofit/repurpose strategy in the next should be strong considerations as you plan your path to success.

At this time, these larger players generally still prefer larger, stabilized assets when they can find them. They prefer to acquire a portfolio of similarly branded and run, medium-to-large assets. They are generally not looking for the mom-and-pops that you will be pursuing in this strategy, but they are looking for the stabilized assets that you will create when you follow this path. That is your opportunity! It means less competition on the acquisition side and a potentially hot market when you sell later.

Mom-and-Pop Review (aka About a Dozen Ways to Increase Revenue)

We covered this before in chapter 2, but it's so important to this strategy that I'm reviewing it again here. Remember that a mom-and-pop self-storage facility relies on oversimplification—or doesn't bother implementing new strategies to increase income. This list will give you a refresher:

1. **If you build it, they will come**: Self-storage units will *not* be automatically occupied just because the facility exists.
2. **Poor online presence**: Self-storage facilities without websites and online marketing will never reach their potential.
3. **No showroom**: This means there are no opportunities to sell ancillary items that create additional income.
4. **Rare price increases**: As we saw in the example in chapter 3, sub-optimal rents can hurt income and value more than expected.
5. **Across-the-board pricing**: Just like hotels and airlines, a savvy operator will price according to demand. Most mom-and-pops never think this way.

6. **Rent what we've got**: Most small operators wouldn't bother with reconfiguring units to meet current demand.
7. **Poor maintenance**: Poorly run facilities are often poorly maintained, which can lead to sub-optimal occupancy and income.
8. **Poor security**: Tenants want to know their stuff won't get stolen. But small-time operators often won't take the effort to install lighting, camera security, and fencing.
9. **No marketing budget**: Small operators often lack the knowledge or desire to advertise. This hurts their occupancy and leaves revenue on the table.
10. **Untapped land**: Sometimes we'll find a facility in a high-demand area that has several acres of extra land that could be profitably used for outdoor storage or more units.
11. **Pest control and water infiltration**: Failure here results in one of the main complaints from self-storage tenants.
12. **Rental truck income**: This is a great source of ancillary income in many markets, but the hassle factor holds many small operators back. There is labor involved, and it's not worth it for many owner-operators.

The Strategy

The strategy is fairly easy to understand. But it takes skill and diligence to pull it off. Here are three major steps:

1. **Acquisition**: Locate and acquire a mom-and-pop facility with clear upsides in the path of progress.
2. **Upgrade**: Clean up and refurbish what is outdated. Modernize systems. Expand marketing and operations. Enlarge facilities. Grow NOI.
3. **Refinance and operate or sell to an institutional buyer**: The increased income will lead directly to an enhanced value. If you're a long-term holder, you will be able to pull out safe equity and operate profitably. If you're looking for an exit, you can take your profits by selling to an institutional buyer. The enhanced facility and a portfolio could lead to a compressed cap rate and an even higher sales price.

Let's explore these three stages.

Stage 1: Acquisition

You'll start this process by determining what you are looking for. Factors may include:

- Geography
- Location and style
- Storage availability to population density
- Vehicle count
- Visibility
- Demographics
- Current competition
- Future competition
- Size of facility
- Facility construction
- Deferred maintenance
- Unit mix
- Current amenities
- Current technology
- Current marketing program
- Current rents
- Tenant base
- Expansion opportunities
- Access to property management

Let's dive a little deeper into this list.

Geography

What part of the country do you want to focus on? Do you need to stay local? Are you trying to build up a clustered portfolio?

Our funds invest with operators who work nationwide and a few who are trying to build up regional portfolios. We've also spoken to a few who only work in one city. These are all reasonable strategies. If you plan to buy and hold one self-storage facility to generate passive income for life, you may want to consider going local. There are significant advantages to driving by your facility on a regular basis, even if you hire a property management firm to run it.

Location and Style

Do you want a location in an urban area? (If so, you may also want to consider the strategy in the next chapter.) Do you want to locate in a residential area in the suburbs? Is it important for you to be near a college, military base, or apartment complexes? Would you consider a growing rural location that lacks current competition? What about a location near outdoor recreational sites?

If you choose an urban location that is densely populated, would you consider a multistory facility with freight elevators? If the facility is in a recreational or more rural area, is there a place in your business plan for outdoor RV and boat storage?

Storage Availability to Population Density

This is one of the most important metrics in your analysis. Regardless of where you consider investing (ground-up, value-add, repurposing, etc.), you need to examine this ratio as a primary consideration. Note that if you plan to invest in self-storage passively, you should analyze this number for yourself. Make sure your operator has evaluated this carefully, and don't excuse it away if it's not in line.

The national average equilibrium density is about seven square feet of storage for every person in a given radius (say three, four, or five miles). The size of the radius may be proportionate to the population density in that area. Look for a smaller radius in a large city (say one to two miles) and a wider radius in a suburban (say three to four miles) or semi-rural area (say five to ten miles).

Draw a circle with a four-mile radius around the location of interest. Check the population in that circle. Check the total square feet of storage in that circle. If the number is well above seven, you should consider passing. If the number is well below seven, you may have a good location. If the number is in the six to ten range, you may face a tough decision. (In general, I would pass on such locations, unless there were other compelling factors like high population growth and favorable barriers to entry against competition.)

To look more closely at this ratio, you should consider regional averages and even add local considerations. While the national average is about seven square feet per person, regional averages can vary. In states like Florida and Texas, there are virtually no basements, and the summer heat is so intense that attic storage is challenging. The average square footage per person may be much higher in these areas. The opposite may be true for midwestern states like Ohio, Indiana, Illinois, and Michigan.

Most people have basements and attics—and they use them. Storage demand may be less than seven square feet per person in these areas.

While we are on the topic, here is a graphic from the 2020 Self Storage Association Demand Study indicating that many self-storage tenants have basements, attics, or garages—and yet they will still spend money every month to store their belongings in a separate unit.

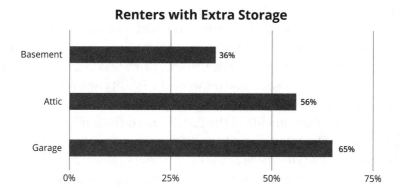

Renters with Extra Storage

Is the area affluent? Is there a lot of recreation in the area, and do people store their RVs, boats, and related toys? This should factor into your analysis. The great news for you is that all this important information is available online. Services like RadiusPlus.com and SpareFoot.com provide helpful data and analysis tools. These online tools can also provide insight into local competitors and help you analyze the propensity for homes in the area to have basements (for storage).

Even though this online data is helpful, and reviewing the area on Google Earth is great, there is really no substitute for driving the area in person. You may see competitors who aren't online and get a sense of important trends. Please don't skip this step in your analysis.

Vehicle Count

You may be in an area with great demand, but is the facility on a popular street with lots of traffic? You need a lot of eyes on your location—and vehicle traffic is key. Though more and more self-storage tenants are finding facilities online, the No. 1 source of new business is still drive-by traffic.

The desired vehicle count is situation-dependent, but many operators want to see a vehicle count in the tens of thousands per day. I know of a great facility with 10,000 vehicles per day passing by. Another location has 33,000 per day. Both work well based on their specific situations and other competitive factors.

Visibility

This may seem self-evident, but it's not enough for your location to be on a highly traveled thoroughfare—it also needs to be highly visible from that road.

We recently invested in a facility that sits way back from a highly traveled road in Greenville, South Carolina. It was a true mom-and-pop, but had more than 90 percent occupancy, which was a great sign. They had an unused acre or so of land between the facility and the road. Some passersby said they had never noticed it. This provided a perfect opportunity. The operator acquired the facility with the land, and now he's in the process of adding a beautiful showroom, an office, and expanded climate-controlled storage near the road. The operator will be able to add signage and achieve great visibility along this important thoroughfare.

Demographics

You'll want to check the income levels in the area as well. Though people of all income levels rent storage, it is obviously better to be in higher-income submarkets. I would hope to have incomes above the local average at the least. A careful local analysis is critical: Be sure to drive up and down every major street in a several-mile radius.

Current Competition

Are the competitors mom-and-pops or national players? How is their marketing? What is their occupancy level? What are their rates? If there is local competition, it's ideal to be in an area of mom-and-pops, especially if you have a superior location or can create better marketing. If you have institutional competitors nearby, however, they may be able to reduce their rates and drive you out of business. On the other hand, the presence of national players could mean you are in a good location. Take all this into account as you make your decision.

Future Competition

This can be complicated. You'll want to check local zoning. It's also a good idea to visit www.RadiusPlus.com to see if they report any planned facilities (they often do). Ask the local building department about currently permitted facilities, and be sure ask competitors and people on the street if they know of any planned expansions or new competitors.

We recently invested in a great self-storage facility on a main road in the heart of a growing residential and multifamily area near Minneapolis. The zoning had been changed, and future competitors would have to be located inside industrial parks. This would be a distinct disadvantage for them and a great advantage for us. There were no permits for other new construction at the time.

QUICK INSIGHTS

Site Visits

Last year, Wellings Capital was about to invest with an operating partner in an existing self-storage facility. Two days before we were to pull the trigger, I made a site visit. The facility was mostly as advertised, but as I drove the area and spoke with competitors, I found one nearby national player that was doing a significant expansion. This bothered me, so I dug deeper. I spoke to another operator who informed me that a large new facility had recently been permitted on a nearby busy corner.

I drove there and saw that the facility was more than permitted: It was under construction—and it was massive. It could crush our facility. This confirmed our belief in the demand in this location, and we had already spent a few thousand on legal fees (document preparation). We could have justified moving forward, but the operator had been unaware of the new construction, and he pulled the plug on his deal. We didn't wind up investing. I'm so glad I made that trip—and so was the operator.

Size of Facility

You need to figure out what size of facility you want to buy. There a lot of factors to consider when making this decision. How much debt do you qualify for? How much equity do you have available? Do you want to self-manage or acquire a facility that can justify hiring a manager? Do you want to contract with a national or regional property manager?

If you're local and plan to self-manage, facility size is not as important. You can manage a 10,000- or 100,000-square-foot facility. But if you plan to have a third-party, fee-based manager or hire your own employee, you will probably want to check to see what minimum size makes sense. Fee-based management firms have a minimum revenue or size threshold. I would say that you'll want to be in the 35,000-square-foot or higher range for most.

I spoke with Tron Jordheim of the Store Here brand, a third-party property management firm. Tron looks to manage facilities that have a minimum of about $15,000 in gross monthly revenue; $25,000 to $30,000 makes the decision easy.

A problem can occur when buying an underperforming asset or one that you plan to expand. If it is physically large enough for a third-party manager but only 50 percent occupied, you might not find a manager willing to take it on. If the facility is too small but you plan to expand, you may be below the size threshold on day one. The solution could be to hire a part-time employee or self-manage initially until you get up to the level that would support a management firm or full-time employee.

Facility Construction

Some older facilities are constructed from concrete blocks or other materials that are either unattractive or don't allow flexibility to change unit sizes. This may not be a deal-breaker, but please be aware of this when you decide on the facility's value. It's important to keep in mind that this will impact resale, and, thus, your total return for the project.

Deferred Maintenance

Construction materials can play a role here as well. For example, a shingled roof might need to be replaced at some point. You may need gutters. There may be water runoff that is impacting stored tenant property. Do a close inspection to be sure you aren't inheriting a lot of deferred maintenance and other costly problems.

Unit Mix

How does the current unit mix compare to the demand in the market? Is it easily changeable (by moving walls)? How many units are climate-controlled versus non-climate-controlled? Are you willing to move walls to change the mix? Do you have room to expand the facility to add the ideal unit sizes and types?

Current Amenities

This is a double-edged sword. You should look for a facility that has short-falls—opportunities to upgrade for optimal profits. But you need to be sure that the space and the zoning will allow you to add what you need. For example, you may want to add truck rental as a profit center. This is a great way to drive additional NOI and occupancy with little to no capital expense. But you'll need a truck parking area and local staff to pull this off.

Current Technology

Look for facilities that are low-tech. They provide an easy opportunity to upgrade to improve operations and marketing.

We looked at a mom-and-pop self-storage facility near Raleigh, North Carolina, last year. We asked about the accounting system, and the owner pulled out a pencil and a handwritten ledger. She went on to tell us that she didn't accept credit cards or online payments.

She was missing a major opportunity. Many self-storage tenants set up payments on auto draft or on a credit card then rarely think about it again. One investor told us he decided on self-storage because he suddenly recalled that he had been auto-paying for a storage unit for seven years.

We asked the owner about her website and she said, "I don't need one. My facility is full." She probably didn't know that her rents were way below market.

Current Marketing Program

Many mom-and-pops are terrible at marketing. Some still rely on a phone book ad! Even more than a low-tech facility, an undermarketed one can offer a great opportunity to increase value and income by increasing occupancy and rents.

Current Rents

Speaking of rents, this is obviously one of the major opportunities you have to increase income and asset value. Many mom-and-pop owners become friends with their tenants. They are frequently happy with the money they are making on their long-paid-off storage facility and are often charging well below market, especially in light of the new marketing programs and other upgrades you will bring to the facility.

I know of one owner whose policy stated, "Whatever rent you start with is your rent for life." This was a great customer-retention strategy.

But it also meant that his revenue and value were below par—a great acquisition opportunity. Think about the power of below-market rents for a moment. Assume the total operational costs of managing a facility are 34 percent, and they can be maintained from the prior owner to the new one. The NOI is 66 percent of the prior gross revenue. Any percentage raise in rent will increase income by a higher percentage, and this will elevate value even more.

Here is a simplified example on a unit basis. Assume the mom-and-pop owner is leasing a 10 × 10 unit for $100 per month. This is under the market average. You take over, and you raise the rent by 25 percent to $125. The cost to manage that unit remains the same, at $34.

The net income on that unit was $66. Now it is $125 − $34 = $91. And $91 / $125 = 72.8 percent. The income percentage is raised from 66 percent to almost 73 percent.

Now assume this increase is applied to 500 units. The former income was $500 × $66 = $33,000 per month, or $396,000 annually. At a 6 percent cap rate, the value of that facility is $396,000 / 0.06 = $6,600,000. (That is your theoretical purchase price.)

The new income is 500 × $91 = $45,500 per month, or $546,000 annually. At the same cap rate, this leads to a new value of $546,000 / 0.06 = $9,100,000. This is a healthy $2,500,000 increase in value; that's more than a 37 percent increase in the value of the asset. This is no surprise since the net profit went up by over 37 percent as well (from $66 to $91 per unit).

But here's where the power of commercial real estate is manifest. If the buyer had 65 percent leverage on the purchase of the property, that means the purchase consisted of $4,290,000 in debt and $2,310,000 in equity (plus closing costs and fees, so assume about $2,500,000 in total equity). By adding $2,500,000 in additional value from this rent increase, *the operator just doubled the value of the equity!* And this doesn't include value-add opportunities like truck rental, expanding the facility, retail items, and more.

Tenant Base

Is your facility populated by price shoppers looking for the best deal, or tenants who care about the location, quality, and safety? Are they students relocating to the area?

One of our favorite operators is obsessively focused on this issue. I didn't see the point at first, but he convinced me. He said one of his first goals is to clear out tenants who are all about price. He's happy for them to go to competitors. Then he systematically markets to less-price-sensitive tenants. He looks for those relocating from higher-priced metro areas and states (like California).

His managers are trained to make conversation with tenants to find out their motivations. These casual conversations can help the operator understand the prospective tenant's tolerance for future rate increases. This operator also uses social media and other online marketing techniques to target just the right types of tenants.

Expansion Opportunities

Many mom-and-pop facilities were constructed when land was plentiful and cheaper, so a lot of these target facilities were built in sleepy suburbs that are now in the path of massive growth. The operators often have no motivation to maximize income and value, and excess acreage is frequently unused or rented out for boat or RV parking. While that's not a bad thing, building a nice showroom or climate-controlled storage facility on this land is generally more profitable.

A mom-and-pop facility we recently reviewed was using only about half of its land. It was on a major road, but the office and storage were set way back. The facility and signage weren't easily visible, and the most valuable part of that land was not even in use. This was a perfect target for expansion. A beautiful climate-controlled facility with a showroom could be built in front. This would be a significant upgrade, creating much higher income and value.

Another operator we know acquired a facility in Baltimore, Maryland. It had no land for expansion, but the local storage market was undersupplied. Without disrupting current tenants, the new operator showed me his plans to add a second story to each building, effectively doubling the square footage. (I don't know if he ever completed this project.)

It's also possible to expand by acquiring neighboring property. Our fund just invested in a facility on the East Coast that sits on a side street about a half a block from a major four-lane thoroughfare. The new operator acquired a parcel of land between the facility and the thoroughfare. It will give the operator space to add a new showroom, signage, an office, and hundreds of climate-controlled units. The operator also has the benefit of current knowledge. They are designing the unit sizes to match present-day demand.

Access to Property Management

This won't apply to everyone, as there are many ways to manage a self-storage asset. Some operators manage themselves. Others hire an employee to run their facility. I recommend you consider contracting with a professional fee-based property management firm, then get out of the way to let them manage.

These firms are typically regional or national—and many are REITs. Is the facility you are considering large enough to support a third-party manager? Is it in an area that has property managers like this? Note that you should consider a location where there are two or three management company options. You will want to have choices if one of them doesn't perform. Sometimes the REIT/manager will be the ideal acquirer for your facility, which could be an opportunity for you to get a compressed cap rate (equals higher sale price).

Now that we've covered what to look for during the acquisition stage, let's talk about how you can do your due diligence when it comes time to acquire a self-storage facility.

Due Diligence

Tron Jordheim offers the following 18 tips on performing due diligence for the acquisition of a self-storage facility. He encourages buyers not to start the (typically) 60-day timeline from contract to close until each one of the agreed-upon due diligence items has been provided by the seller.

1. **Current rent roll**: Review it carefully. Sometimes names and units get mixed up. Also look for phantom tenants and side deals the owner may have with friends and family. This can take a bit more effort than multifamily, since you can't see inside each unit. Make sure you recheck the rent roll again before closing. One of our operator friends acquired a facility that had about 40 units "rented" by family and friends who proceeded to leave right after closing. This was hard to detect up front, and it really hurt financials for quite a while.

2. **General ledger for past three years**: Look for fake revenue and unreported expenses. Try to locate patterns and blips. If the past 12 months are stellar and the prior 24 were awful, that should raise some red flags. Or it may show you that the market has really taken off lately.

3. **Monthly P&L for the last 12 months**: See if this raises questions.

"Why no landscaping costs?" Nonreported items can be typical of mom-and-pops due to family doing free work, or maybe the owners are simply sloppy recordkeepers.

4. **Historical occupancy for three years**: Look for the owners adding a lot of occupancy in the past few months. This may mean large concessions or a "friends and family scam."

5. **Examine all capital improvements**: Some of these haven't had improvements in decades. Bake in allowance for extra repairs and renovations in old facilities. Try to come up with a list of potential repairs as well as capital expense improvements before finalizing your capital raise and debt structure.

6. **Third-Party management company**: Talk with the current management company and ask employees about their experience in the area and at the property. You may get leads to other deals as well. And if they're sloppy, this may show you an opportunity for improvement when you take over.

7. **Current insurance**: Are they overinsured? Underinsured? Look for opportunities here.

8. **Current real estate tax bill**: Talk to a tax assessor directly, and talk to their boss, assistants, and others. Find out if there are errors in the tax records, and ask about the likelihood that the bill will go all the way up to a percentage of the full purchase price level. Check this number over and over because if you make a $50,000 mistake, that amounts to almost $1 million in value at a 5 to 6 percent cap rate.

9. **Review all tenant leases**: Can they be modified, or will you need new leases from each tenant? Make sure there's a lock on the door for every lease on file.

10. **Review recent survey, appraisal, phase I, site/engineering plan, building plans**: Are all of the buildings noted on the drawings? Are property lines where they appear to be? Where is the flood plain and what happened the last time there was a flood?

11. **Check 12 months of utility bills and compare to P&L**: Don't accept: "We don't have access to those bills." You may be able to get the information directly from the utility company. Look for what was spent in the hottest and coldest months. Look for issues with insulation, temperature controls, etc.

12. **Advertising**: They may have spent zero on ads, but recall that their cost basis is way different from what yours will be. They may have

purchased the asset for a fraction of the current cost and have little to no mortgage.

13. **Service contracts**: Review all contracts for maintenance, janitorial, pest control, lawn, etc. Look for issues with bed bugs, mice, termites, and such. Snow removal can be a killer. Guess this number wrong, get hit with a few heavy snow years, and it can crush your NOI. Is there room to push snow? If not, snow may have to be hauled away! This is why some don't buy in New England—their NOI could be wiped out with snow removal.

14. **Tax returns**: If they won't show the tax returns, this is a huge red flag. Sellers may make misrepresentations on their offering memorandum or proforma. Sellers can do this in many ways. This is a negotiating tool for a buyer, however: "My lender needs to see the tax returns." People are less likely to fudge numbers on tax returns. Try to review three years of the seller's Schedule E (Form 1040).

15. **Have the accountant/CPA sign off**: Make sure you have the accountant or CPA's signature on all this information. They're not likely to sign off if they suspect any information is fraudulent.

16. **City**: Check for violations, what is filed, etc. Do they have a permit for boat and RV storage?

17. **Competition**: What else is planned and zoned for the area? Who is building and who is expanding? Have other new self-storage applications been turned down? That can create barriers to entry for competition, which would be great. Gather all possible information.

18. **Physical inspections**: Hire a professional who knows self-storage. Check roofs, water paths, Phase I environmental, and surveys.

Speaking of physical inspections, you may want more details on what to look for when you inspect a property. Here's an abbreviated 12-item list provided by self-storage investing expert Scott Meyers.

Items to Scrutinize During On-Site Tours and Inspections
1. **Gates and fences**
2. **Lighting**: Visit the property at night to ensure that lighting is in working order.
3. **Water drainage**: Look for water marks on and inside units.
4. **Doors**

5. **Signage**
6. **Overlocks**: Overlocks are locks that the manager can place over the tenant's lock if they haven't paid rent. Check how many units have these, and ask how many tenants pay late. Compare records. If it is late in the month, that could really be a problem, which could be your opportunity to ask, "How often do you hold auctions?" (We recently invested in a Dallas facility where 28 of the 240 or so units had long-term nonpaying tenants. The prior mom-and-pop owner was too lazy to conduct auctions. Our operating partner was glad to buy the facility, conduct an auction, and free up these units for rentals—a great profit opportunity.)
7. **Building protection**: Do they have bollards (protective posts)? These are useful to protect the corners from bad moving van drivers. Don't accept damaged corners—consider renegotiating the price to repair them.
8. **Roofs**: Shingles are inferior to steel.
9. **Temperature**: In a climate-controlled facility, the industry standard is 55 to 85 degrees, with no HVAC until temperature gets outside that range. Some mom-and-pops maintain a temperature of 72 degrees, which is a waste.
10. **Lighting inside units**: Bad idea. People plug other things inside these units, like refrigerators, and it can be a liability. Units should be constructed in a way that doesn't require interior lighting; hallway lights will be sufficient to illuminate the interior of the unit.
11. **Exterior units**: Check doors, interior construction, lip on door, seals on door, etc.
12. **Land for expansion**: Look for parking and other opportunities to expand.

Establishing a Rapport with the Current Owner

When Warren Buffett acquires a company, he recognizes that it's someone's baby. He makes a lot of effort to ensure that the owner/seller feels good about him, his company, and how operations will progress in the future. Sometimes the owner/seller takes less than top dollar to guarantee they will have a legacy.

You need to be acutely aware of this when you are speaking with potential sellers. Treat them with respect and take opportunities to compliment them on what they did right. The days of insulting the seller to beat them down on price are over—as if that ever worked anyway.

Brokers will argue that this is a good reason to have a middleman, which may be a good idea. Sometimes it's hard for a buyer to avoid insulting a seller when attempting to get the best price and terms. Whether you use a broker or not, treat the owner/seller with great respect and make sure the feeling is mutual.

Matt Ricciardella of Crystal View Capital has a team of five to seven acquisition specialists who work the phones day in and day out, calling owners to see if they wish to sell their self-storage facilities or mobile home parks. Matt's team acquires over 90 percent of their deals off market. How does he do that? Matt treats sellers with respect and deference, and though they realize he's not necessarily paying them top dollar, they feel cared for and honored in the process.

Here's the proof: In Matt's previous $10 million fund, 35 percent ($3.5 million) of the investments came from owners/sellers. They actually took funds that he paid them and reinvested them with Matt's company.

That's powerful testimony to the golden rule: "Do unto others as you would have them do unto you." It's also a far cry from the alternative I heard in my early years in the business: "Do unto others... and then run!" (I think that was a joke—at least I hope so.)

Stage 2: Upgrade

Once you've acquired a mom-and-pop self-storage facility, it's time to upgrade. I've covered many of these upgrades by implication in this book, but I will do a brief overview of 18 items here. Upgrade opportunities are numerous and dependent on the situation.

1. Use road frontage
2. Clean up/refurbish (corner guards, fences, locks, gates)
3. Install security and lighting
4. Modernize systems (collection, accounting)
5. Add truck rental
6. Offer free moving truck for move-in
7. Provide free shelving
8. Offer insurance
9. Charge administration and late fees
10. Add ancillary retail sales
11. Expand facilities
12. Provide boat and RV storage

13. Put up a billboard, cell tower, propane station, ATM, etc.
14. Enforce timely evictions
15. Improve marketing (signs, web, social media, geotargeting, remarketing, move-in specials, etc.)
16. Price by demand
17. Size by demand

Use Road Frontage

Have you ever said, "I've been passing that place for years and never noticed it"? It is critical to acquire a facility with great frontage on a busy road. But your visibility must also be maximized on that road. This may mean adding signage, building a new office/showroom, adding more storage, or even acquiring adjacent land. Using the frontage is your first order of business.

Clean Up/Refurbish

This is your second order of business. This may include new paint, roofs, gutter guards, doors, fencing, gates, etc. It could include patching asphalt and restriping parking spaces. It will almost certainly include adding bollards to guard corners against rookie moving van drivers.

Interior changes may include a major showroom overhaul as well as improvements to the office and counter area. Think about the colors and layout of the showroom and the path from the front door to the counter. You will also want to repair dented walls and corners in the storage area and add corner guards here as well.

This step may also include securing the physical property and land: ensuring that water runs off properly, buildings aren't rusty, and the property is not being damaged, deteriorated, or corroded in any way.

Install Security and Lighting

Mom-and-pop facilities are often poorly lit and not well secured. If you came to this location, would you feel safe? If you were alone in a long interior corridor, would you worry about who was around the corner? Upgrade the paint colors, add motion-sensor LED lighting (inside and out), and ensure that the showroom, grounds, and interior storage all look inviting and secure at all times. A well-lit parking lot, showroom, and signage can be a boon to advertising.

Modernize your security. Consider adding a large, multipanel screen in the office so visitors can see that the facility is under constant surveillance. Add systems to allow you to monitor which tenants are on location at all times, and be sure all prospects and tenants know about it.

Modernize Systems

Mom-and-pop operators are notorious for poor accounting and collection systems. These can be upgraded. While your goal is to make all your prospects think about you as much as possible, ironically, it is often an operator's goal to make sure tenants don't think of you much at all after they're a customer. Make sure you've set up systems that allow you to collect rent via credit card and ACH (automated bank withdrawal).

Add Truck Rental

Providing truck rentals (like U-Haul or Penske) can add a nice chunk of revenue to your operation with little cost to you. One of the operators we invest with has a facility in Florida that generates up to $5,000 in monthly commission from renting U-Hauls. Since many people who rent trucks also need storage, it is likely that truck rentals will also increase occupancy and ancillary sales. Operators often report increased occupancy of about 3 to 5 percent, which is a big deal.

Offer a Free Moving Truck for Move-In

You may not have the space to park several trucks, or you may be surrounded by other U-Haul or Penske dealers. In that case, you may want to acquire one moving truck, brand it for your facility, and offer it free to incoming tenants. This branded truck can also advertise your free offer. Operators who do this typically provide free truck rental only for the first day so they can also generate revenue for longer rentals. Tenants who move out have to pay for its use as well. (Note that you can do both third-party truck rentals and a free moving truck.)

Provide Free Shelving

Some operators offer free shelving to tenants. This typically costs only about $100 and can be assembled in about an hour. It can be part of the advertising in your showroom. Tenants with shelving will be able to store more stuff and have another reason not to move out. You could also elect to charge a nominal fee for shelving, which would provide additional revenue.

Offer Insurance

Stuff happens. Tenants' treasures can be damaged by mold, water, heat, or bugs. It is in everyone's best interest for you to contractually require that each tenant have insurance on their contents. You can offer an insurance option that will provide you with revenue sharing, but please note that you cannot require tenants to buy insurance *from you*.

Charge Administration and Late Fees

Many small operators don't charge these types of fees either by policy or omission, but you can do so. Consider charging a nonrefundable administration fee rather than a refundable deposit. This will probably be more profitable for you in the long run. Very few tenants damage their units, so most would receive their deposit back. If they pay an administration fee instead, they will be out the same amount up front and you get to keep the funds in the end.

QUICK INSIGHTS

Value-Adds

You may not think that items like insurance, administration fees, and late fees will add much to your bottom line. However, it's not just the income but the added value that counts. Remember our commercial real estate value formula:

Value = Net Operating Income / Cap Rate

Assume your revenue share from insurance is $5 per month. And assume that you have a 60 percent sign-up rate on 1,000 units. That's 600 units × $5 per month × 12 months = $36,000 in increased income. That's wonderful.

How does that impact value? At a 6 percent cap rate, it could look like this:

Value Increase = $36,000 / 0.06 = $600,000

Let's continue this example. If the facility cost $10 million, your (yet unrealized) value increase just went up by 6 percent to $10,600,000. But it's better than that. If you purchased the facility with 70 percent

LTV debt, the original equity was $3 million. The $600,000 increase went straight to equity, increasing the equity value by 20 percent.

That's 20 percent equity appreciation just by adding insurance netting you $5 per month, making this is one of the easier, least costly value-adds.

Add Ancillary Retail Sales

Those who rent self-storage and moving vans have predictable needs for retail items. You should profit from selling them. These include a variety of moving boxes, tape, scissors, and locks. Sell these in a stylish showroom and you may be able to add a thousand dollars per month in income. Using the commercial real estate value analysis, this could result in an additional 10 percent or so in equity appreciation, and you may draw in more clients too.

Expand Facilities

Expansion is one of the most profitable strategies for adding value and growing equity. Many mom-and-pop owners sell with a decent amount of vacant or underused land included. Sometimes adjacent land can be acquired as well. Many times, the old drive-up storage in a great location can be profitably augmented with the addition of more visible and lucrative climate-controlled self-storage.

By adding on a lovely showroom and office with attractive signage, a mediocre facility can be upgraded to a highly profitable REIT target. By moving both the numerator (up) and the denominator (down) in the value equation, this single improvement can result in massive investor returns. This opportunity should be high on your list of potential modifications.

Provide Boat and RV Storage

Though it is often more profitable to add buildings on vacant land, there is also profit potential in boat and RV storage. This could include parking for work trailers, semi-trucks, and other vehicles.

I recently toured a new facility that is providing boat and RV storage. One of the team members told me his friend pays $190 per month and drives 30 minutes to store his RV in an unsecured gravel lot with no electricity. By providing fencing, security, a paved lot, and an electrical outlet, the new facility is projecting fees of $225 or more for oversize parking spots. 20 spots at $225 = $54,000 annually. At a 6 percent cap rate, that's a potential value of $900,000.

Put up a Billboard, Cell Tower, Propane Station, ATM, etc.

Think about what other profitable uses for the land might be available. You may be positioned to develop a powerful income stream to augment your facility's income by including one of these items on your land.

Enforce Timely Evictions

Some mom-and-pop owners are pretty lax. It's a hassle to evict. Many are busy cutting their grass or enjoying the beach, and it can be easier to let late tenants slide. But once they start down this slippery slope, it can be hard to get back on track. By holding tenants accountable to timely payment with the threat of eviction, you'll be happier and run a more profitable facility.

One of the facilities we recently invested in had 80 percent delinquency when it was acquired from a mom-and-pop owner. After consistent enforcement, delinquent payments have decreased to only 5 percent, which is about the industry standard.

QUICK INSIGHTS

Timely Payment

A friend of mine recently acquired a mom-and-pop facility that previously accepted only checks and cash. The owner-manager invoiced each tenant monthly by mail. Then tenants had a week or two to mail in payments or drop off cash. Some of them even left their payments inside their rental units, asking the owner to open their doors to retrieve them. (Yes, seriously.)

My friend had one particularly frustrating tenant. The tenant didn't like the new owners and called them regularly just to complain. "Why do I have to pay by credit card or ACH? I will pay you 14 days after receiving an invoice in the mail. Or I'll slip the payment in my unit for you to pick up. By the way, can you explain again why you raised my rent? And why I can't pay by cash? And how do you expect me to get my payment in on the first of the month?"

Eventually my friend had had enough, and he evicted the tenant.

The well-located facility is 100 percent occupied, even after 30 percent rent increases. He told the guy to move out by the end of the next month. The hassle was not worth his payment.

Improve Marketing

This is one of the most effective potential improvements for most mom-and-pops. As mentioned earlier, many owners take the *Field of Dreams* route, relying on people to show up just because the facility is there. Decades ago, that used to work.

A facility I just heard about has no Google listing, virtually no signs, and no online or offline ads, but they were virtually full. This speaks to below-market rents. It also indicates that there may be room to implement many online and offline strategies to drive up revenue, profits, and value.

Marketing strategies may include tactics like rebranding, new signs, new colors and logo, updated website, social media strategies, pay-per-click marketing, geotargeting, geofencing, remarketing or retargeting, move-in specials, community outreach, or joint ventures.

Price by Demand

I walked into a Florida self-storage facility and asked, "Can you tell me about your pricing?" After fishing around in a pile of tools, folders, and assorted papers on the counter, the man pulled out a disheveled copy of a copy of a copy of an old price sheet. It looked like it had not been updated in years. He crossed out several unit sizes that were sold out. Clearly the thought of adjusting pricing by unit demand was a foreign concept. Classic mom-and-pop behavior.

We are all familiar with the experience of sitting on a plane next to someone who bought tickets early at half the price we paid, or double. It's the same for hotels and dozens of other products and services. When you're nearing full occupancy for any unit size, consider raising the price on that size. There are certainly other factors to be considered, but pricing by demand should be on your radar.

Size by Demand

The next step is to alter unit sizes to meet demand. We're talking four pieces of sheet metal, a door, a floor, and some rivets—pretty basic. For example, you could remove an interior wall between two 10 × 10s to create a 10 × 20 for a client, or add a wall to create two units out of one.

I was at a new facility recently that is built on five-foot sections throughout. This facility is set up in advance to expand or contract unit sizes to meet demand, so it will be better positioned to meet unknown future customer requirements. And that may make it more attractive to an institutional acquirer.

Stage 3: Refinance/Operate or Sell to Institutional Buyer

Once you've progressed through the first two stages, your facility should be stabilized and running well. It's time to figure out what to do next—and the answer will depend on your motivation.

Refinance and Hold

Do you want to hold the facility long term? Have your efforts led to a significant increase in the value of the facility? Are you comfortable safely raising the debt level to pull out principal to invest elsewhere? If so, it may be time to consider refinancing.

We've talked about many ways to raise the facility value. If you started with 70 percent LTV debt, you may be down below 50 percent after a few years of improvements. By adding a supplemental loan or refinancing with a new loan, you should be able to safely give the principal back to yourself and your investors. The money is returned with no tax consequences and allows a single "principal seed" to grow into two "asset trees." This is a powerful approach for multiplying your capital.

Sell to an Institutional Buyer

Would you rather maximize your IRR and ROI by selling sooner? Do you have investors who require an early exit? Do you need a complete cash-out to do other projects? Is your facility positioned to sell to a REIT or another institutional investor? Is it part of a portfolio of facilities that can be marketed together? If so, you may want to market your facility to an institutional investor.

In general, institutional investors are looking for stabilized, low-risk, low-hassle assets. They are looking for deals where most of the heavy lifting has been done and are willing to trade appreciation for a stabilized, predictable, steady yield. They are often willing to buy at a compressed cap rate (high price) in order to achieve these objectives.

If this is your ultimate goal, please take this into account in the acquisition phase. REITs don't want to buy in Podunk towns or out-of-the-way rural areas; they don't want to buy small facilities, and they don't want to buy where they have no other assets and no management team.

REITs *do* want to buy in areas where they already have management, and sometimes they're even willing to buy in oversupplied markets. They like to buy commonly branded portfolios and, as I said, they will trade appreciation and ongoing yield for stability and lack of hassles.

Selling to a REIT has the goal of compressing the denominator in the commercial real estate value equation. Though we've discussed this before, it bears reiterating. In the following scenario, assume for a moment that you are buying from a mom-and-pop and selling to a REIT—an arbitrage opportunity where you do nothing to increase the numerator (NOI) in our value equation. This is not realistic, but I want to restate a point about the power of compressing the cap rate.

Let's say you buy the facility at a 7 percent cap rate and you sell it to an institution at a 5.4 percent cap rate (which is realistic). How does this impact value? If the NOI is $500,000 in each case, the value is calculated as follows:

$$\textbf{Purchase Value} = \frac{\$500,000}{0.07} = \$7,142,857$$

$$\textbf{Sale Value} = \frac{\$500,000}{0.054} = \$9,259,259$$

$$\textbf{Difference} = \$2,116,402 \text{ (an increase of 29.6 percent)}$$

By now you know there is more to this story. If you financed your purchase at a 70 percent LTV, your original debt was $5 million, meaning your original equity was $2,142,857 (plus some acquisition costs). This equity is 30 percent of the purchase price of $7,142,857.

Your gain in value of $2,116,402 went straight to the equity, almost doubling it. Yes, your purchase at 7 percent and sale at 5.4 percent nearly doubled your equity, with over 98 percent equity appreciation from this one act (compressing the cap rate).

Is compressing the cap rate really doable? Absolutely. One of the operators we invest with has done it on 21 deals in the past few years. Their investors achieved 40-plus percent IRRs in the process. Of course, the increase in NOI is a major part of the equation too. And that makes it much better than double.

A Value-Add Success Story

Our Wellings Income Fund invested in a self-storage asset in a western U. S. state last year. This formerly mom-and-pop asset was acquired and operated by Matt Ricciardella of Crystal View Capital. Matt's four acquisition team members each call about 150 to 200 self-storage and mobile home park owners and managers on a daily basis. Their goal is to drum up off-market transactions.

One of Matt's team members, James, made contact with the owner of the facility, who seemed nervous but admitted that he wanted to sell. James connected him with Matt, who started a conversation with him. The owner explained that he had been the owner and manager for a very long time, and things were not going well. Though he had 80 percent occupancy, his delinquency rate was also running at about 80 percent. So, four out of five tenants were not paying on time and some had fallen months behind.

As Matt got to know the man, he figured out why: He was neurotic, fearful, and overbearing. He had apparently alienated the tenant base, and they learned that they could pay late (or not at all). Matt visited the facility and recognized many problems that are typical of mom-and-pop self-storage assets:

- Extreme delinquency
- Subpar occupancy
- Below-market rents
- Years of deferred maintenance
- Poor record-keeping
- Virtually no systems
- Shoddy customer service

Some sellers don't want to use a broker and are ashamed to even meet with a potential buyer. Why? Often, it's due to books that are in disarray. This may include some under-the-table revenue they don't want to disclose—but want to be credited for when calculating the value.

It became clear why the seller didn't go through a broker when Matt saw his books, which were written with pen and paper and were a mess. Matt had to convince his banker on the upside potential of this asset, since the revenues were light, and the expenses were heavy. After a lot of wrangling and suspense, the acquisition finally closed a few months later.

Over the first six months, Matt and his team created value by:

- decreasing delinquency from 80 percent to 5 percent;
- increasing occupancy from 80 percent to 92 percent;
- increasing gross revenue by 17 percent;
- overhauling the branding, which created a new image and enhanced the customer experience for existing and new tenants;
- replacing the front gate, adding rebranded signage and new landscaping, and resurfacing multiple sections of the asphalt;
- adding U-Haul truck rentals, which increased monthly income by $3,900 and helped to drive traffic and, in turn, rentals to the facility;
- generating 50 new move-ins in only four months, with the help of online marketing through SpareFoot or a similar service;
- building an online marketing presence via a website and Google, which has generated significant traffic; and
- hiring a new management team with outstanding customer service and sales skills, that have executed the management strategy quickly and efficiently.

Note that some of these items are not traditionally considered value-adds. Landscaping, resurfacing, and new signs can fall under the category of deferred maintenance and beautification, which sometimes are just necessary items. But in this case, with the new management's desire to completely overhaul the image of the facility, these are part of a great value-add strategy. And they supported the team's program to show existing tenants they needed to pay or lose their stuff. And this boosted their ability to raise rents, acquire new tenants, and add ancillary revenue like U-Haul and showroom sales.

Speaking of U-Haul, consider the value added to the facility by signing and implementing this truck rental agreement. Revenue of $3,900 monthly is $46,800 annually. When applying our value formula (value = NOI / cap rate), this translates to a value increase of $720,000 at a 6.5 percent cap rate. By increasing rents and occupancy plus convincing past tenants to pay (or face eviction) as well, this turned out to be a home run deal.

This 650-unit facility had been acquired for $4.3 million. At that time, the net operating income was $295,322. By implementing these strategies, Matt's team raised the facility's NOI to $456,891 in only six months. This translates to a projected increase in value of $2.3 million, from $4.3 million to $6.6 million, or even better if the cap rate can be compressed. Since the original debt on the facility was about 50 percent, this means the equity was about 50 percent as well ($2.15 million in raised equity). This $2.3 million increase in equity translated to a 107 percent increase in the value of the equity—*in only six months*! This shows the power of this strategy.

The facility is projecting a cash-on-cash return from operations of 21 percent and a 47 percent IRR. If operations go according to plan, the property will generate a 4.2 MOIC—320 percent total profit—in four years to be shared by investors and the operator. By the way, the prior owner of this asset has now offered to sell Matt another self-storage asset. They are in negotiations as I write this.

The previous example is a great way to create a wealth-generating career for yourself if you want to do real estate full time. If I were starting out in commercial real estate, this is the course I would strongly consider.

But some of you don't have the time to fully focus on a strategy like this one. If you're busy pursuing a full-time career or enjoying retirement, perhaps you should consider investing passively in deals like this, with a fund or an expert operator who knows how to find anomalies. Sharing profits like this by just walking to the mailbox has made thousands of investors very happy. As I've often asked myself and other investors, "Why work harder than necessary only to make less than you could?"

CHAPTER 8

SUCCESS STRATEGY 3: RETROFIT AND REPURPOSE AN EXISTING BUILDING

Many U.S. industries have been moving offshore for decades, leaving empty factories and warehouses across the fruited plain. And the online revolution has resulted in the shuttering of thousands of retail centers. Kmart, Sears, and Toys "R" Us are three of the major casualties, but there are many more.[23] The pandemic of 2020 only accelerated the process.

I recently passed a shuttered Kmart at Addison and I-94 in Chicago, Illinois, and wondered how many similar empty buildings populate this large city. They are nearly all in great locations on well-traveled roads, which can often make them a great target for retrofitting and repurposing. Self-storage is a potentially great use for these empty buildings! The

23 Hayley Peterson, "More than 9,300 stores are closing in 2019 as the retail apocalypse drags on—here's the full list," Business Insider, Dec 23, 2019, https://www.businessinsider.com/stores-closing-in-2019-list-2019-3

location and most other acquisition criteria will be the same for this strategy as for the prior one. But instead of acquiring an existing operation, you will be looking for an empty building with the demand and location criteria that will allow you to create an outstanding self-storage facility.

Retrofit Building Requirements

When evaluating potential properties, there are some definitive requirements, some negotiable characteristics, and some features that are bonus qualities for this type of retrofit. I will break them down for you into those three categories. This list was compiled with the help of my friend Scott Krone, an experienced self-storage operator at Coda Management Group, who has done a number of successful retrofits. Note that some of these items are particular to his firm's strategy.

Definitive Requirements
- **Solid demographics**: Visible location, density, level of competition, rental rates, etc. (This is the same as any other self-storage deal.)
- **Size:** 70,000 to 110,000 square feet.
- **Floor-to-ceiling height:** 11 feet or more.
- **Structure:** Needs to be able to carry 125 pounds per square foot for live and dead load.
- **Acquisition cost**: Below replacement cost of structure. Scott often acquires old buildings in urban areas in the range of $10 to $20 per square foot.
- **Access**: Need approximately 5 to 10 parking spaces, as well as the ability to drive a car into the building and back a truck up to a loading dock area (limited parking needs is another aspect of self-storage that I love).

Negotiable Characteristics
- **Zoning**: Prefer the property to be properly zoned, but if not will need to assess the level of difficulty to entitle the property.
- **Configuration**: Can be multiple story—the more rectangular, the better.
- **Structure**: The more regular, the better. Columns are preferable to load-bearing walls.
- **Mechanicals**: MEP (mechanical, electrical, and plumbing) can be

assessed. Optimal to have existing fire suppression and other utilities.

- **Other features**: The ability to lease space for cell towers, billboards, ATMs, and other revenue-generation sources.

Bonus Features

- **PACE**: Certain states provide property assessed clean energy (PACE) incentives. PACE is a Department of Energy program (implemented at the state and local levels) that provides financing to spur green buildings and efficiency. Any improvements made to increase the efficiency of the building can be financed through an approved PACE loan. Repayments for debt from the PACE program are applied directly to real estate taxes and not to the loan, so it is an "above the line" expense. Therefore, banks view it as equity instead of debt.
- **Opportunity zones**: At the time of this writing, there are significant benefits to acquiring and redeveloping a property in an opportunity zone. Opportunity zones were created in the 2017 tax bill to provide developers and investors incentives to invest in economically challenged areas. (I'll go into this more soon.)
- **Historic tax credits**: Properties that have unique historic features that can qualify for credits are a bonus.

A Powerful Retrofit Example

Scott and his team did a successful project that fit most of these criteria in 2018 in Toledo, Ohio. After the success of this project, they went a few hours south to look for a similar opportunity in Dayton this year.

Scott teamed up with a commercial broker who knew the market. He found three possible sites for Scott to evaluate. They settled on 535 Third Street in downtown Dayton for a number of reasons. The building had 90,000 square feet, five stories, and a full basement. Ceiling heights ranged from 11 to 14 feet. The building was rectangular and was a poured-in-place concrete structure with columns. It easily exceeded the 125 pounds per square foot load-bearing requirement. The building already had two loading docks. One had the capacity to be reverse-ramped so tenants could back their cars into the first floor.

Surprisingly, Scott was able to acquire the property for only $11 per square foot. Obviously, this was well below construction cost. Another bonus: The property was already zoned for self-storage. Since it was an old building, it was certainly far from move-in ready. It required all new MEP, a new roof, new windows, and a fire suppression system.

When I first heard about it from Scott, I assumed the column structure would be a hindrance to the future layout. Scott is an architect, and he said the columns actually provide more flexibility. There are four elevators in place, two of which will be converted for use at the facility. The other two will be converted to mechanical shafts.

This sundae has two cherries on it: The property is in an opportunity zone, and it qualifies for PACE financing. These two financial features dramatically amplify investors' projected ROIs.

PACE financing fits in the middle of the capital stack between debt and equity. The debt on this project is 70 percent loan-to-cost. In a typical project, this would mean that the equity required would be 30 percent.

In this situation, the energy improvements qualify for 15 percent in PACE financing. With 70 percent traditional debt plus 15 percent PACE, Scott only had to raise 15 percent in equity. This effectively means that any increase in value will have a much higher than normal (perhaps double) impact on equity.

This is a pretty staggering multiple. Let's consider some simple math here.

First, recall our commercial value formula.

Value = Net Operating Income / Cap Rate.

Every dollar in monthly income adds up to $12 in annual income; $12 in annual income at a 6 percent cap rate results in $200 in value ($12 / 0.06). Typically, with leverage of, say, 66.7 percent, this would have an impact on equity at a 3x multiple over the return on the total project (100 / (1 − 0.667)). In this case, the impact on equity is *6.67 times* (100 / 1 − 0.85): over double the impact. This means that a given percentage appreciation at the asset level will result in 6.67 times that appreciation at the equity level.

If Scott can drive up income 10 percent, the asset value increase will be 10 percent. But this 10 percent appreciation could result in equity appreciation of over 66 percent (6.67 × 10%). This seems almost unfathomable, even to me as I write it. But this is the power of leveraged commercial real estate, and in particular a deal like Scott's. It gets even better.

The opportunity zone means that investors can delay taxes for years, and in some cases avoid capital gains taxes altogether. This is not meant to be an exhaustive explanation of opportunity zone fund tax treatment. But here is a brief overview of three categories that an opportunity zone investment may fall into, assuming that Scott's company is able to meet all the necessary qualifications.

1. If Scott holds the investment for five years and does not roll it over into another qualified opportunity zone project, his investors could receive a temporary deferral of capital gains from a previous investment. This prior investment could be real estate, stocks, bonds, etc.

2. Scott's investors could receive a step-up in basis of 10 percent on the reinvested assets if he holds the new investment at least five years plus an additional 5 percent if the asset (or fund) is held for seven years or more. Therefore, either 10 percent or 15 percent of the original gain is excluded from taxation.

3. Scott's investors could receive a permanent exclusion from taxable income of capital gains from the sale or exchange of this opportunity zone investment if the investment is held for at least 10 years. This exclusion applies only to gains accrued from the investment in this asset (not prior investments that were rolled into this opportunity zone investment).

Scott set up an opportunity zone fund that will allow him to potentially roll over from one asset to another if it is optimal to sell this Dayton asset in less than 10 years. His goal for this project is to refinance after about three years, return investor equity, then hold for three to five more years.

Scott models costs on a project like this to come in at only about 65–70 percent of a newly constructed project. He projects that the resale price at the end of the line may be slightly lower than new-built due to inefficiencies inherent in the layout of an older building. This discount is lessened when the building has a regular shape, as this one did.

Lesson learned: PACE financing and opportunity zones, when applicable, can have a major impact on increasing value and lowering taxes.

Make Your Move Wisely

Should you go out and find an existing building to retrofit? Maybe—especially if you have a background in construction or resources to assist you in this arena.

You may wonder, as I did, what the first step is. Should you look for a demographic hole or find an appropriate abandoned building? I think either one could be a good way to start. But I want to warn you that it's easy to get emotionally caught up in a deal and start to ignore the facts. You know what I'm talking about: confirmation bias.

A friend once found an abandoned brick factory in Cincinnati, Ohio, for under 10 cents per square foot. It was in a gentrifying location, and the city was willing to provide incentives for him to acquire it and turn it into a self-storage facility. Would this be a good investment?

First, it was on a major, heavily trafficked road. It was five stories tall and highly visible. Second, it was located in a quickly gentrifying neighborhood that had recently turned from a dangerous area into an urban hipster destination. New multifamily buildings, restaurants, and retail locations were springing up all around. Third—and very important—we checked the RadiusPlus website, which showed the most useful radii were usually three, four, or five miles. In an urban location like this, perhaps a two- or three-mile radius would be most helpful.

The goal, as we've discussed, is to be in a location where there are less than about seven square feet of storage per person in any given radius; however, that is a national statistic, which could be different in certain localities. For example, demand will probably be higher in places like Florida or Texas, where there are no basements, and lower in the Midwest, where basements are commonly used for storage.

We were happily surprised that the statistics showed only about three-square-feet of storage per person in a three-mile ring. My friend was getting excited and it seemed that confirmation bias could be setting in. We toured the facility again, and he was almost ready to put in an offer. His next step was to consult with an experienced operator who had done two or three of these conversions in the past. This operator took him through a checklist similar to the one previously mentioned. Sadly, this facility failed on numerous counts.

First, the load-bearing capacity didn't appear to be up to par. It would need to be reinforced. Also, the shape of the building was irregular. Parking was a problem and so were the locations of the elevators. And there were countless other issues as well.

I wondered whether the confirmation bias would get in the way and he would plow forward anyway. Fortunately, we set aside emotions and made a smart decision. He walked away and started looking for another building in the area.

How to Make a 700 Percent Profit in a Coma

Remember AJ Osborne, who I mentioned back in chapter 4? I want to share a self-storage success story he told as a guest on the *BiggerPockets Real Estate Podcast*. AJ and his team purchased a Kmart in Reno, Nevada, a few years back. The first thing they did was sell off the parking lot to a multifamily developer for $3 million.

The second order of business was to cut the building in half. After beautifully dressing up the entrance, the team went to work converting the interior to self-storage. The facility had 125,000 interior square feet and room for exterior storage as well. The structure, floors, ceiling, roof, electrical, HVAC, and parking were all in place. It was already in a great location on a well-traveled thoroughfare. Zoning was easy to change, and there was a structure in place for signage.

In the middle of the process, AJ went into a coma. He had contracted Guillain-Barré syndrome, and it was touch and go for months. AJ's team pressed on, though, and the facility was completed and opened on time. They had about $7.5 million invested in this project. This consisted of about $5 million in debt and $2.5 million in equity. When AJ was last on the show, they were in the lease-up phase. He predicted that this facility would be worth over $20 million when they achieved full stabilization (about 90 percent occupancy) in a few years. In the best way possible, he was mistaken. Later that fall, AJ was expecting an offer from a REIT on the property soon.

On a recent call with AJ, I asked him, "I thought you were only 40 percent leased up. You're not even halfway to stabilization, right?" He responded that the location, their successful business model, and the speed at which they were leasing up was drawing significant interest from institutional investors. Before our call ended, AJ had received an offer of $25 million on his facility, directly from the buyer with no brokerage commissions. Let's do the math: His $7.5 million net project cost consisted of $5 million in debt + $2.5 million cash.

If he took this offer, he would net almost $20 million after paying off debt. That's a $17.5 million gain on a $2.5 million investment, a 700 percent cash-on-cash profit in about two years—not counting any cash flow along the way.

Is this normal? Certainly not. Is it possible to replicate? I don't see why not. The fragmented nature of ownership in the self-storage arena and the opportunity to repurpose empty buildings are providing a unique window of opportunity to build projects that will benefit the community, profit investors, and build your wealth in a major way.

SECTION III

SEVEN PATHS TO SELF-STORAGE MASTERY

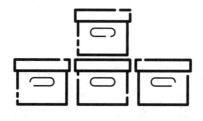

CHAPTER 9

PATH 1: THE LONG AND WINDING ROAD

This is probably the most obvious route to large-scale success in self-storage, but it may be the slowest. Because of the monotony and time involved, it could ultimately turn out to be the hardest too.

It's been said that ordinary things done over and over lead to extraordinary results. I put this path first because I believe that sentiment and because this "obvious path" can be used as a benchmark that other paths can be compared to. In their epic book, *The One Thing: The Surprisingly Simple Truth Behind Extraordinary Results*, Gary Keller and Jay Papasan discuss how truly prosperous people must endure the monotony of success. They're talking about the fact that many successful people get clear on their goals, then endure the painstaking, often grueling monotony of doing the same tasks over and over for decades to achieve those goals.

They avoid chasing shiny objects, and they're willing to press on when mundane tasks get boring. They learn to say no to a thousand distractions along the way. Their endgame is so crystal clear in their vision that they are able to endure where so many others fail.

Who Is an Ideal Candidate for this Path?

Keith Cunningham is a great business leader. He is known for paying his tuition for success in the form of making, then losing, then making back about $100 million over his lifetime. Cunningham teaches that ordinary efforts, applied consistently, over and over again, produce extraordinary results. He teaches that there are no secrets to success, no magic bullets. His opinion is shared by many of the super-successful investors.

If you believe this and are the type of person who can pull it off, you may be a great candidate for this path. It calls for a person who is resourceful, patient, and handy. At some point, they also need to learn how to delegate effectively, which is a skill that every entrepreneur must learn on the road to mastery.

Though it's not necessary, I believe that such a person may have a great opportunity to involve their family in the business. Most of the other paths I describe may have limited opportunities to involve family members, but this one provides the opportunity in spades, as you'll see in the story later in this chapter.

If you are sold on self-storage and want to build an empire but you have no contacts in the business, have limited experience and capital, and lack other resources to get in the game, this may be a good path for you to travel.

You May Be Ideally Suited for This Path if You...

- Are willing to put in the time and effort to learn every facet of this business.
- Are a hands-on, do-it-yourself kind of person.
- Have the patience to grow your business step-by-step over many years (or decades).
- Have the capacity to acquire debt and bring your own cash to the table (or have access to it).

Journey

A lot of real estate investors start out with single-family rentals, and they have a goal of amassing a portfolio of 20 properties, 100 properties, or more. As I detailed in my previous book, this is a recipe for burnout for most investors, especially those who manage their own properties.

Even those who don't self-manage typically recognize the superior economies of scale available through larger-scale commercial real estate investing. As I mentioned previously, the superior value equation for commercial real estate allows operators to "force appreciation" and significantly multiply ROI.

In the case of those who graduate to multifamily, it's one roof for many units: one (huge) yard to mow and maintain, one place to plow snow, one convenient office for many tenants, and multiple sets of eyes and ears in one location to look out for potential crime, maintenance issues, and unhappy tenants.

That's why many single-family investors soon make it a goal to jump up to duplexes, triplexes, or larger. Most eventually realize they want to operate commercial-level multifamily properties.

This is all well and good, but as I've previously stated in this volume, multifamily (at the time of this writing) is overheated, and the market is not at all fragmented. Therefore, many multifamily wannabes and even current operators are finding it hard to get in or to expand.

Most of the successful self-storage operators and investors I've met started off in single-family flips or rentals, then graduated (or tried to graduate) to multifamily for a while. But once they realized not everyone had the knack for finding multifamily deals, discovered the power of a fragmented market, and the variety of value-add opportunities available in self-storage, they made the jump. This is similar to the path I took.

After converting from single or multifamily (or something else) to self-storage, there are several typical steps to take on this first path. Though I must generalize, here are a few you might follow.

1. Acquire a small self-storage facility that (hopefully) has some glaring deficiency. This may be a local facility that has 50 or 100 units, is 10,000 square feet, and is something that you can acquire with your own funds or those you pool from friends and family. (I mentioned elsewhere that I don't think starting small is an ideal path. But my goal here is to provide options, and this is certainly a legitimate one.)

2. Fix it up. Upgrade or improve the facility in various ways (operationally, physically, marketing, etc.).

3. Take strategic steps to prepare to increase rent, decrease expenses, and increase tenant quality and/or occupancy, thus, increasing income. This may include building extra units on vacant land, or at least renting unused land to RV and boat owners.

4. Rent it out (or boost rents). Increased income drives increased value.

5. Sell the asset for a profit or refinance (to release cash). If you are able to refinance with cash out, you may reduce your effective investment in the asset to zero (or even less). Selling the asset will release the most cash to "cascade up" to the next property.
6. Locate a larger asset and repeat the process.

By naming these steps, I'm obviously leaving myself open to the possibility of criticism. Virtually no one's path will follow these exact steps. But hopefully this will give you a general idea. BiggerPockets readers may recognize this path. It sounds very similar to the widely quoted BRRRR strategy:

1. **B**uy
2. **R**ehab
3. **R**ent
4. **R**efinance
5. **R**epeat

You're probably wondering, "Should I hold on to all these rentals and pay down/pay off the debt?" You would think so: It seems to be the natural path to wealth. When people first consider acquiring rentals, they hear about the concept of letting tenants pay off their mortgages while they sleep with the goal of eventually having a large stable of assets that produce income and no mortgage payments.

It sounds like a great strategy, and honestly, it is hard to criticize the idea of being out of debt and having dozens or hundreds of cash-flowing units. But is this the best strategy for achieving the highest level of income and wealth? Probably not. In his book *The Complete Guide to Buying and Selling Apartment Buildings*, Steve Berges discusses two strategies that apply just as well to self-storage as to multifamily investing.

The *buy and hold strategy* is effectively buying and operating rental properties with the goal of paying off the debt over a number of years, then continuing to enjoy the income for years to come.

The *buy and sell strategy* means that the operator buys a property, makes meaningful value-add improvements, increases income, then sells it for a profit. They repeat the strategy over and over, using increased equity to buy a larger apartment building each time.

Note that neither of Berges's contrasting strategies truly considers refinancing and holding properties while using the equity to buy the next one.

Value-Add Opportunity

Though I haven't seen this definition anywhere else, the simplest way I can quickly explain the value-add opportunity is this: Buying an asset that has a given, known ROI, and then improving some aspect of the property in a way that the ROI *on the improvements* is much higher than the ROI on the asset as a whole is one way to meaningfully raise the average ROI on the entire project.

A buyer of a value-add asset recognizes some meaningful shortfall in an asset and spends the money and time to make improvements that raise the rents and net income on the property, making the asset more valuable as a whole.

Value-add improvements are a way to "force" appreciation of a commercial real estate asset. This is not achievable in the residential real estate world, since the value is derived by comparable sales rather than by income and the cap rate.

In Berges's buy and hold strategy, the investor starts with $20,000 in cash and buys one $100,000 property per year (with 80 percent LTV debt) for 10 years. Then they hold all 10 rental properties for 15 more years, ensuring that the debt on all of them is paid in full by the end of the 25th year. The example assumes annual appreciation of 4 percent along with a few other reasonable assumptions.

The result is that the investor amasses a respectable stable of debt-free homes that will generate a comfortable retirement. Total value = $2,162,232.

You may think, "This is very doable. I'm going to go do that!" First you may want to check out Berges's alternative strategy, one that reflects the path I'm recommending in this chapter.

In the buy, upgrade, sell, repeat strategy, the operator effectively starts with the same $20,000 and acquires a single $100,000 rental property with 80 percent debt. But this operator takes quick action to add value and increase the rent, then sells the property for a $20,000 profit at the end of year one.

They take the total equity of $40,000 ($20,000 original + $20,000 created by value-add strategy) and acquire a new $200,000 asset with 80 percent debt. The operator does the value-add and sells that property a year later for a 20 percent profit. They acquire the next $400,000 property with $80,000 down and $320,000 in debt.

They proceed to repeat this process for 10 years, and like the buy and hold investor, hold the last property in the chain from year 10 until it is paid off in year 25. Assuming the same growth rate of 4 percent annually and—with the significant effort and tenacity—repeating this process annually for 10 years, this operator will have generated a value of... wait for it...

$92,208,307 by the end of year 25.

I will concede one major point. While I'm fine with Berges's 4 percent appreciation (and I'm fine with creating 20 percent in value-add appreciation), I question the likelihood of being able to repeat this cycle annually.

As commercial properties get larger in size (the sixth one was $3.2 million and the tenth and final one would be acquired for $51.2 million), buyers are more focused on seeing a year of increased rental income history, and base their purchase price on that. Therefore, I think that spacing out the process over a few years is more achievable.

I haven't run the numbers with two- or three-year spacing for the last several cycles of Berges's buy and sell strategy, but I can tell you that his point is correct: The buy, upgrade, sell, repeat path (that I'm generally advocating in this chapter) will probably beat the buy and hold path by a wide margin.

A Word on Managing Properties

One caution: Path 1 has a real risk of LLF, or landlord fatigue. It's the natural outcome of owning and operating your own real estate assets. Being your own property manager is very challenging, to say the least—especially if you're a nice person and tenants realize they can take advantage of you. It seems like a no-win situation for most because not being nice brings its own challenges. There are certainly gifted people who can walk the line of firm, fair, consistent, and kind, but they are rare.

The good news is that Path 1 does *not* require you to manage your own properties. I make this point because I believe that the type of person who would attempt this grueling path would be the same type of person who would attempt to manage their own properties long term, someone who doesn't naturally delegate and who is willing to invest sweat equity to put more cash in their pockets. It can be done, but it could be challenging.

By the way, regardless of your path, it's a great idea for you to self-manage at first or to self-manage a few small properties along the way. The experience is extremely valuable once you move to the role of asset manager (overseeing other property managers) when the time is right.

Path 1 in Action

A guy called me from Dallas asking for advice on acquiring a 19,000-square-foot storage facility he found for about $1.1 million. It had a neighboring parking area that could be acquired to expand the facility. The issue: He didn't have the capital to acquire a facility by himself, even though he had experience in running other, larger facilities.

I mentally reviewed the seven paths, and it seemed clear that Path 1 was the best for him. This acquisition was probably about the right size to get him started. Although it was too small for an on-site manager, he could run it himself (he lived nearby and had the experience). If he could upgrade it to a larger, more profitable facility then sell to a larger player, he could create equity and get on this path.

A more dramatic example comes from the multifamily realm but is worth mentioning anyway. I met an apartment owner in Arlington, Texas, a few years ago. He was selling his 130-plus unit complex for about $11 million and planned to move up from there or retire. He owned it mostly for cash.

He started on his path 22 years before by using a $1,000 bonus from work to acquire a duplex. He fixed it up, rented it out, and made $400 monthly for some time. At some point he realized this was not the road to riches, and he sold it for a $25,000 profit.

He did this repeatedly over the course of 20 years, increasing the size of almost every acquisition. That's how he wound up with the $11 million asset, and he likely traded up to a $16 million asset after selling that one.

Another example comes from a man named Tim Puffer. Tim and his wife had gone to a number of guru seminars, and they eventually bought a duplex. They assumed this would be the first step on their path to a larger portfolio or to cascading up, as we've discussed in this chapter. But managing this single duplex was not as easy as they had heard. The tenants were constantly complaining about things they had already fixed more than once. One weekend they were at another guru seminar in Cleveland, Ohio, and their phone was lighting up with tenant complaints. They were tired!

About that time, someone across the table leaned over and announced that he had just discovered the "glory" of self-storage, and he was selling his rental homes to make the switch. Tim and his wife decided to do the same. They acquired a small self-storage facility near their home in Lansing, Michigan. Tim says that operating this entire storage facility was easier than dealing with the duplex he'd had before. He explains that the lack of toilets, flooring, plumbing, lighting, and live-in tenants (he had about 200) in his self-storage made all the difference.

Is this the path you want to take? Do you have the skills, patience, and determination to climb this tall, grueling mountain? I can't promise that your experience will be similar to Scott's and Tim's, but this is a workable path for the right person.

CHAPTER 10

PATH 2: BAPTISM BY FIRE—THE FASTEST PATH UP THE STEEPEST MOUNTAIN

This chapter is for those with access to a lot of capital—that is, cash—be it your own or that of others in your circle who would trust you to make good investment decisions. Perhaps you:

- Just won the lottery
- Have an inheritance
- Sold your tech company for a big profit
- Own or run a family office
- Have the courage and the network to do a syndication
- Sold your Bitcoin at the top of the market before it plunged 50 percent in 2021

Whatever your situation, you'll need a good amount of cash to make Path 2 work. You will have to:

- qualify for a large commercial loan (unless you're buying all cash);
- convince a commercial broker that you're the best buyer;
- convince the seller that you're the best buyer and/or be one of the highest bidders;
- have a great credit score, high net worth, and high liquidity.

As I said, much of this can be achieved through the syndication model, and many of you may want to go this route. But I warn you: If that's your plan and this is your first rodeo, you need to ask yourself (and your investors) if it's a good idea for you to pursue this path with no (or limited) experience. Syndication often works best in concert with one of the other paths (in other words, once you have already walked one of the other paths for some time, and have the experience to successfully syndicate a deal).

QUICK INSIGHTS

What is a Real Estate Syndication?

A real estate syndicate is a group of investors who pool their capital to buy or build property. Combined, individuals and companies have more buying power than what they could easily manage on their own. Syndicates are commonly structured as special-purpose entities, such as limited partnerships or limited liability companies. Despite the legal form it takes, a special-purpose entity is the method by which investors purchase the real estate, such as an apartment complex, office building, or even a portfolio or property fund.

Who Is the Ideal Candidate for This Path?

As I mentioned before, this chapter is mainly geared toward those with significant net worth or access to capital—those who realize that commercial real estate is one of the best paths to sustain and grow their wealth on a tax-advantaged basis. If this is the path you want to pursue, it is certainly the fastest way to the top. But unlike the previous long and winding road, it's more like a climb up a steep rock face. It is possible to do this as a rookie, but you'll need some great guides and safety equipment.

You May Be Ideally Suited for This Path if You...

- Are a quick learner.
- Experienced in business.
- Able to delegate and outsource.
- Resourceful and courageous.
- Have access to a lot of capital.
- Have access to loan guarantors (or you are one).

What Are the Rewards of This Steep Climb?

My first mentor told me that when I had capital, I would have access to a lot of profitable, wealth-propagating opportunities that are not available to the general public. I also learned that those with capital are good targets for scammers and less-than-experienced and less-than-scrupulous operators. I hope you won't fall prey to them. If you are in this situation, there are certainly many potential benefits to just jumping into large-scale commercial syndication right away. I'll contrast this path with the others.

- You won't have to endure the very long and winding Path 1. You will immediately have access to the many benefits of large commercial real estate.
- You won't have to accept a fraction of ownership, as on Paths 3 and 4.
- You won't have to punch a clock or "work for the man," like those on Path 5.
- You will have control of ownership, unlike those on Path 6.
- You won't have to pay a coach or endure the delays of Path 7.

What Are the Challenges to Expect on This Steep Ascent?

A Significant Learning Curve

Occupancy and rent assumptions, marketing goals, and staffing plans are all subject to the baptism by fire in the furnace of real-world market dynamics.

Even veterans can get fooled. A knowledgeable developer I know is building a beautiful, top-dollar storage facility in a growing market. He had the land and was pursuing approvals. He never expected an abandoned Sears store would be converted to a storage facility down the road.

His aesthetically pleasing facility will likely be outgunned by the more economical refurbished retail space nearby.

Winning Over Brokers and Lenders

As I said earlier, this may be no small feat. Commercial brokers don't have to present every offer, and they will generally select buyers whom they know will close without hassles and retrading, even when the offer is lower. They usually have a group of friends they sell to over and over. You will have to convince them they should choose your offer. That may come at the price of a higher offer or high nonrefundable deposits—not usually a great strategy for success. They may even see you as a sucker, and then your multiple purchases with them could turn out to be a curse for you.

Commercial lenders have a fiduciary responsibility to their employers and capital sources to carefully underwrite the buyers. This means ensuring that there is adequate net worth and liquidity to make payments if things go south, and to potentially rescue the deal in extreme cases. This is true whether the loan is recourse or nonrecourse. It also means that the lender will be vetting the operator to ensure they have the experience and the team to pull this off. This can include asset managers and an experienced property management team. Don't assume that your capital will compensate for this important requirement.

Overly Competitive Market

The investment world has discovered the potential of commercial self-storage, and it is unlikely that the next downturn will change this fact. At the time of this writing, many markets are overheated. Cap rates are compressed to all-time lows (expensive!), and some operators/investors are going to get burned. Regardless of the strong demographics and recession resistance of self-storage, there are still local dynamics to deal with.

If you are new, you may be tempted to unknowingly overpay for an asset in an already oversaturated market, as is happening in many areas across the United States. That is why you need a good team that includes a trustworthy person who will tell you that your idea might be a bad one.

What Will This Path Require from You?

This path will likely require the most concentrated effort from you in a short time period. Don't assume anything. You will need to immerse yourself in books, podcasts, mastermind groups, and other training. I recommend that you get involved on BiggerPockets and make meaningful connections.

You will want to do quite a few property tours and learn how to do your own underwriting. You will need to learn what to look for in due diligence and assemble a team to help you with this. No one will care as much about your money as you do, no matter how well you pay them. Though a lender may mandate repairs upon closing, there may be many things they miss or don't mandate. Make sure to look for problems that will cost you money later.

How Do I Get Started?

You'll likely need more than $1 million in light of net worth and liquidity requirements, as we discussed in chapter 5. That chapter may be worth reviewing now if you're fuzzy on the details.

Of course, you'll want to be sure you qualify for debt. Don't wait on this step. By getting prequalified early, you will know whether you can move forward or how you will need to bolster your team first.

My main piece of advice is to build a great team around you. Do not try to do this alone. Buy in a market with multiple large property managers and interview them all. Also consider partnering with an experienced asset manager, someone on your team who will help you along every step of the process. A great asset manager could help you select a lender and a property manager up front and hold the property manager accountable for financial and operational performance over the long haul.

You may be able to find a co-asset manager from the world of mentors, which I cover in Path 7. That's what my company did when we were newer in the multifamily space. We would never have been able to navigate the prepurchase items or the first year of operations without them. I'm sure it could be done in a deal with a lot of meat on the bones, but those deals are hard to come by.

Loan Guarantor or Earnest Money Provider

I want to throw out one more pair of options on this path: the opportunity to become a general partner in a deal by cosigning on the loan and the opportunity to put up earnest money deposits for syndicators who need financing.

If you're a person with both cash and wisdom and you want to jump into commercial real estate, this could be a good avenue for you. You see the wisdom of getting into this profitable arena, but since you're wise, you may also realize that you don't currently have the knowledge you need to grow your own self-storage or commercial real estate portfolio. One way to do this is by finding a great syndicator who is upgrading their deal size but doesn't have the net worth and liquidity to sign on a large loan. You could cosign for their debt or put up their earnest money.

Let's talk about signing on the debt first. What are the steps?

1. **Get to know the syndicator:** This is more than a phone call or two. You need to meet them in person, see their past deals, talk to their investors, and more.

2. **Analyze their team:** Be sure that all of them, including their property manager, have the skills, experience, integrity, and commitment to pull this deal off.

3. **Meet with the lender:** Be sure their only hesitation with the deal is the cosigner with the net worth and liquidity to meet their requirements. Try to negotiate a nonrecourse loan, which will usually limit your liability to fraud and the introduction of environmental hazards at the property.

4. **Personally analyze the deal:** In person. And hire someone who really knows the business to critique it. Make sure you like the geography, the submarket, and the asset. Insist on a third-party review of the project.

You will probably want to know what percentage of the ownership you will get for signing on the loan. Don't shortchange yourself here. This is a valuable service you're providing, and you deserve to be well compensated. Even if the loan is nonrecourse, you are still taking on liability by signing on this debt.

As I mentioned, another profitable function that often goes hand-in-hand with being a loan guarantor is putting up the risk capital. That is, for example, the deposit and some of the costs to undertake due diligence before closing. This can be risky, and if you put down cash at this point, you deserve a disproportionate equity stake for your investment. In other words, if you put down 5 percent of the equity, you may want to ask for, say, a 10 percent equity stake if your capital is at risk.

There's probably a lot more that you need to know to follow these subpaths, but I just want to plant these thoughts in your brain to get you started.

A Real-Life Investor Who Took This Path

As I said earlier, this path is best suited to those who have the courage and the network to jump right into a syndication. It's impressive for anyone to do this; it's especially impressive when the investor is in his 20s.

James Reid is that guy. I met James at a self-storage mastermind group, and I knew he was a man on the move. I asked James to tell us his story:

Big Dreams

While I was in high school, I owned and operated a landscaping company. One of my goals was to be a land developer and real estate investor. As I grew the landscape company, with sales of over $1 million, I knew the scalability would be challenging with a service-type business. I started investing in rental property right after high school to start my journey into real estate investing. Once I was in rentals, I started to research self-storage, knowing this was where I was going to grow as a developer and investor.

Strategizing

Planning for a business in storage spaces has been a rewarding process. I had big dreams, and even though we had no site yet, I was building a business plan. I started to reserve cash from my rentals to prepare to buy or develop a self-storage facility.

I bought domain names and hired a trademark attorney to help me trademark StorCo. I wanted to learn as much as possible, so I joined the Missouri Self Storage Owners Association.

I also attended every Inside Self-Storage (ISS) show to meet storage professionals and kept a journal to track everything I was learning.

Searching Every Day Pays Off with an Unbelievable Find

As part of my business strategy, I began evaluating storage properties all over the Midwest. In 2016, I started to investigate conversion opportunities with vacant box stores, like old Kmarts. It took a while, but by December 2017, I'd found a listing on LoopNet for a vacant Chevy dealership in Wood River, Illinois. It included 15 acres, three storefronts, one office building, and a used car sales building in the front lot. The buildings totaled 93,000 square feet.

The property was listed for $990,000, and it already had $90,000 in annual rental income (a 9 percent cap rate!). At first, I thought it was not a real listing, so I called the agent, who confirmed it was real and the price was accurate. I saw immense potential in this property, and I knew it would be a great opportunity for self-storage. I called Marla Colic, my agent, and we sent an LOI at the asking price.

The Offer

The seller moved very slowly. We were still not under contract four months after my offer. The main building had been vacant for over five years, and we ordered inspections for all the buildings on the property. As a result of the inspections, I adjusted my offer to $500,000, and we ended up agreeing on a final sale price of $550,000, which was 55.5 percent of the list price.

Don't Always Assume What You See and Hear Is True

During the time of sending the LOI, I was seeking out banks to lend money on the property. One bank had a lot of interest in our project and promised a 60-day close. I proceeded to follow the bank's process.

The seller's agent gave us a clean Phase I environmental report on the property, which was required by the bank. After 30 days of working with the first bank, we still did not have an engagement letter guaranteeing that they would go through with the loan. A week later, I received a call from the bank informing us that they would not be able to fund in time for closing. They did, however, provide references for other banks, and I began to explore each one.

Things Get Messy

As we submitted documents to the new banks, they flagged the clean Phase I environmental report as unacceptable, so we had to order a new one. As I read through the appraisal ordered from the previous bank, something did not seem right. I contacted an expert to review the appraisal, and he found that it was inaccurate. Therefore, the new bank ordered a new appraisal.

The new Phase I report came back dirty for three reasons. First, there was an old gas station on-site, but there was no documentation stating that the tanks had been removed. Second, there was a full dry-cleaning operation on-site. Third, asbestos was found in a small portion of the building. It turned out that the first clean Phase I report was only for a small piece of the property, not the whole parcel.

Digging Deeper

With these results in hand, we ordered the more comprehensive Phase II environmental report, which required drilling 60 feet into the ground to see if there was any contamination from the gas tanks. While awaiting the results, I started getting bids from asbestos removal companies. One company said they had already been to the property to give a quote on asbestos removal. This raised a huge red flag as we realized that the owner was withholding information about the property.

During another site visit, I talked to the dry cleaner. She asked if I had been in the back-shop area. I had not, so she showed me the area, which had an additional 4,500 square feet inside the building. Around this time, we received the new appraisal for the property and a clean Phase II report. Despite these obstacles, we were able to negotiate more time to allow the banks to close on the property.

The Right People and the Right Mentors

Mentors have been a large part of my business success over the years. Since people don't know what they don't know, having a mentor can make all the difference. As I was building StorCo, I wanted to find a mentor and connect with the Scott Meyers Self Storage Academy group. They were able to share their experience in the storage-space industry with me. They also held weekly accountability calls with me to work through all the items needed to close on the property and to cover other aspects of self-storage.

Closing on the Property

We received the green light from the bank with all the documents, the clean Phase I and II environmental reports, and the appraisal. I had the cash available and was able to close on the property. My intent was to raise equity to replace part of my cash later.

Raising Capital

We had a great response to our first equity capital raise and raised $500,000 in 30 days. We worked with an SEC attorney to set up the private placement memorandum (PPM). There are several legal documents and reports that must be arranged through an attorney, and finding the right firm is important, both for raising capital and for lining up investors.

The Deal

Property and Buildings	$550,000
Construction	$1,950,000
Total Project Cost	**$2,500,000**
Debt	$2,000,000
Capital Raise	$500,000
Holding Period	5 Years
Equity Partner Ownership	25 percent
Five-Year IRR	19 percent
Total Profit to Investor Group	132 percent
Total Annual Return to Investor Group	26.4 percent
Five-Year Equity Multiple	**2.32x**
Return of Principal to Investor Group	$500,000
Appreciation to Investor Group	$465,527
Cash Flow from Operations to Investor Group	$198,915
Total Proceeds Received by Investor Group	**$1,164,442**
Five-Year Projected Appraisal	$8,100,000
Total Proceeds to Sponsor/Syndicator (James)	**$3,493,328**

StorCo's Grand Opening

We closed on the property in November 2018 and opened the doors for business in April 2019 with an amazing 10-day carnival on-site, complete with six live bands, a beer garden, and lots of fun activities. The event will be an annual occasion called the Wood River Spring Fest, with over 15,000 attendees expected to participate. StorCo also made over $12,000 in profit from the carnival.

Lease-Up Phase

At the time of this writing, we are four months into our lease-up period for the storage facility. We have about 81 units rented out of a total of 503, which is about 16 percent occupancy. The projected four-month occupancy was 7 percent. We are more than double our projections because of StorCo's positive relationship with the city and the community.

A Final Observation

Did you notice anything unusual in James's equity split? If you've been around the investing world long, you may be used to seeing a preferred return with the majority of the split above the return going to the cash investors. Often, you'll see something like an 8 percent preferred return (the first 8 percent to investors), then a 70/30 split in favor of investors. How did James get away with no preferred return and only 25 percent of the equity ownership going to the cash investors?

It's called reverse-engineering the equity split from the return. When your deal is strong enough, you as the sponsor/syndicator can often get better terms for yourself. James started by asking what a reasonable expected return would be for an investor. For a development project like this, it could be an IRR of the high teens or 20 percent, and a total annual return in the low 20s.

Once that is determined, the equity split can be maneuvered to give the cash investors about that much return. In this case, that resulted in James's getting the lion's share of the ownership. He will make a lot of money. If this bothers you at all, recall that James signed on the loan and will have spent about seven years working on this project.

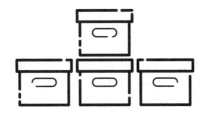

CHAPTER 11

PATH 3: JUMP-START YOUR CAREER AS A SELF-STORAGE DEAL FINDER

Are you convinced about making the jump from your W-2 job or your single-family residential business into self-storage? If so, you're likely also convinced that the best way to own and operate self-storage is to go relatively big. I'm not saying, "Go big or go home." But I *am* saying that the economies of scale in self-storage are often more viable at a larger facility.

For example, the effort and cost of signage, online marketing, and sales efforts may be similar at small and large facilities. A similar cost spread over many more units results in a lower percentage cost at a larger facility.

Another issue regards staffing. If you believe the path to maximum profit includes an on-site staff person for most regular business hours, you'll find that it makes much more sense to own a large facility. Having a staff person can also open the door to U-Haul rentals and retail sales, revenue sources that cannot be achieved at small facilities. A showroom to sell retail items would not be practical at most small self-storage facilities anyway.

It makes sense, if possible, to jump into a large self-storage operation. But that's not always easy to do. That is why this path might be appealing to you. Here's what I like about this path: You can get into a significant facility through this path without the self-storage experience, the team, the cash, the debt capacity, the capital connections, and the full-time effort required to acquire a large facility on your own.

You May Be Ideally Suited for This Path if You...

- Have a lot of time available and are willing to make calls or knock on doors.
- Are limited in capital.
- Are creative and persistent.
- Have direct marketing skills and background.
- Love to talk with people and are a great networker and negotiator.

Why Does the Deal Finder Path Work So Well?

As I write this, we have seen a decade-plus rise—really an explosion—in the popularity of commercial real estate investing.

Commercial real estate investing and self-storage in particular have exploded in the past decade. The popularity of commercial real estate investing has been fueled by the:

- proliferation in commercial investing resulting from internet marketing and social media;
- loosening of syndication investment rules;
- bounce-back after the Great Recession;
- influx of international, IRA, and 1031 exchange investors;
- disenchantment with Wall Street's casinos;
- significant increase in accredited investors;
- over-pricing and over-crowding in other asset types, like multi-family, and;
- entry of institutional players chasing yield.

Question: What does this have to do with the deal finder path?

Answer: These circumstances make finding deals more difficult. *And much more valuable.*

Here's why...

In times like these, when self-storage is increasingly popular and in high demand, there are more operators going after a shrinking pool of assets. Shrinking in the sense that mom-and-pop deals are getting snatched up regularly and new/large facilities aren't candidates for most acquisition programs. Furthermore, a given operator only has a certain reach. They can only check out so many deals, and none of them can easily cover a huge area (many states or nationwide).

Due to the popularity of commercial investing, many operators have far more capital than deals. Investors of all sizes have a lot of cash chasing deals. Great deals are hard to locate and negotiate. And this is where you could play a vital role. This is how you could make your mark and break into this industry.

How Does the Deal Finder Path Work?

A deal finder creates a relationship with an established syndicator/operator. After learning their criteria and negotiating a financial arrangement, the deal finder searches for deals for the operator. If the operator acquires one of the deals, the deal finder has the opportunity to stay involved to learn the business and share in the profits, or at least get a nice payout on the front end.

To pull this off, you would need to find an operator who needs deals and is willing to work with you. Then you would need to figure out a strategy to find off-market (and occasionally on-market) deals. Next, you might need to help get the deal across the finish line. Hopefully, you will have the chance to stay involved with operations and every other aspect of running the facility.

I'm confident you can find operators looking for deals, since finding deals is the hardest part. How can you find off-market deals? Here are a handful of ideas.

- **Driving for dollars**: You can make a map of all of the facilities in your area. Drive them and stop by those that look promising. Many small operators are on-site, and you may get an edge over those who just send mailers and local brokers who contact them. I know one great operator whose acquisition person flies to a different city about three weeks out of every month to do this. He has found many deals that are not even viewable online.

- **Mailers**: You'd have a lot of competition here, but investors still do these because they work. If you catch an owner at the right time with an attractive postcard or letter, you may get their attention.
- **Handwritten letters**: Before you scoff, I'll tell you that my son has been doing this for several years. He hired his sister to do the writing. The response rate is much higher than standard mailers, but you've got to stick with it. This tactic goes well with the next one.
- **Phone calls**: The most successful self-storage operator I know has a team of people calling owners daily. There is no substitute for this type of marketing, but, like the others mentioned, you'll have to stick with it.
- **Online marketing**: If you can get in front of the right person with the right message at the right moment, I believe this could work. But I think it's a long shot for the most part. I would think that social media strategies would be your best shot if you try this tactic.
- **Self-Storage websites**: You may be able to locate a deal on a website targeted to the sale of self-storage assets. A good place to start is ListSelfStorage.com.
- **Local networking**: By getting involved in your local real estate investor association, chamber of commerce, etc., you may learn about operators who want to sell. You can also post on BiggerPockets forums to seek out operators in your area who may be interested in selling. Additionally, it would be beneficial to speak with moving companies, U-Haul dealers, and other self-storage operators to see what they know about those who may sell.
- **Commercial brokers**: Some deals are too small for commercial brokers. They may pass them along to you and ask for a small fee or no fee at all. There are many self-storage brokers, some nationwide, and I would guess that some of the best don't have time for smaller deals.
- **LoopNet and local MLS**: LoopNet is like a national multiple listing service (MLS) for commercial property. It is not popular with investors for a number of reasons. Many brokers and commercial

operators assume that if a deal is on LoopNet, it is either overpriced or has some major problems making it hard to sell. They assume it was marketed by a broker or FSBO and did not sell. Now LoopNet is the seller's last resort. While I would rarely recommend going to LoopNet for deals, there may be occasional deals there that are overlooked by others. I'm also including the residential MLS because I recently heard of an investor who found an underpriced, under-marketed deal from there.

- **Self-storage operators:** Yes, I realize how odd this sounds. But when I worked with a friend to try our hand at being deal finders as a side gig, this is where I got my best leads. Operators who sift through thousands of off-market deals probably discard well over 95 percent. Some of them would be great for another operator, or even for that operator if you can negotiate a better price and terms. If you can get a list like this, it could send you down the path as a deal finder.

I'm going to share two fresh examples of this last tactic. Like I said, a friend of mine and I thought it would be great to drum up some side income using the discarded leads from a successful operator friend of mine. One of them was a large facility in the Pacific Northwest. He had notes from his acquisition team about the details and the likely price the owner would accept.

Upon calling the owner, we learned that the price included a lot of other land around the property. He was developing this land into a valuable industrial park and more. When I told him we had no interest in this other land, he dropped the price to about 60 percent of the original proposed amount. This took the deal from pretty good to fantastic. We got the deal under contract at that price and have a variety of options on how to take it from here.

Another was a self-storage facility in the Southeast. It was inherited, and the children don't live in the state in which the facility is located. The prices were below market, the occupancy was under 60 percent, and the marketing budget was zero. They didn't rent trucks or sell ancillary items. And, perhaps most encouraging, there were 10 extra unused acres that came with the sale. This could provide room for expansion with more drive-up units or even a climate-controlled facility if the market warrants it.

My friend and I have a signed LOI on it and are in the process of placing it under contract. Since my company is a professional investment partner in self-storage deals now, we would not consider operating it ourselves. We will have the option of playing deal finder for another operator or wholesaling it for a nice profit.

Tools for Your Toolbox

If you travel this path, there are a few tools you'll need for your toolbox. First, you will need to become quite familiar with RadiusPlus. This will help you locate facilities, evaluate competition, and more. RadiusPlus provides maps with all competitors in a given radius (say within four miles of the facility). It also provides data on demographics that will allow you to evaluate the ratio of self-storage space to the population in that area.

Second, you will need some negotiating skills. Chris Voss was an FBI hostage negotiator and wrote a wonderful book called *Never Split the Difference*. You can hear Chris discuss negotiating on Episode 206 of the *BiggerPockets Real Estate Podcast*.

Third, you'll also need some great sales skills. Though I don't recommend every one of his tactics, Oren Klaff's book *Pitch Anything* is a classic on positioning and selling.

Fourth, you'll have to put up with sloppy owners with shoddy records. One of the reasons many of these folks don't go to real estate brokers (or lenders for refinancing) is that they fear they can't. Their handwritten records and cash payment systems would take too much effort to reform for public consumption. The same issues you'll have to slog through to understand a true picture of their records are the same issues that could provide you with a great deal. A deal that no one else has uncovered.

Finally, you'll need persistence and patience. I don't know of a book or course on that. You must cast a wide net for most of these tactics. I have a few friends who send out tens of thousands of mailers month-in and month-out, often to the same owners repeatedly. It's a grind. But if you're willing to do what few others will, you'll get the results that few others get. That's just a fact of life.

Some Benefits of This Path

- If you don't have access to millions of dollars or the capacity to raise or borrow this much, this could be a great path for you to be part of a multi-million-dollar deal.

- You don't need training, education, or experience in running a self-storage facility to do this.
- If you don't have relationships or credibility with brokers to get the inside track on marketed deals, you can create your own track as a deal finder.
- If you have a full-time job or you're enjoying retirement and can't devote a full-time effort to this business (at least now), you can still make some side profit.
- If you don't have the time or the propensity to build a self-storage team from the ground-up, this path allows you to tap into an established team with knowledge and experience.
- There's a higher chance for profit and a lower chance of loss on a deal acquired and operated by pros.

Some Practical Tips for This Path

- **Negotiate your deal finder arrangement upfront**: Though an operator may be reluctant to sign a legal document with an unproven deal finder, it is worth the effort to have all of the terms agreed to in advance. It would be easy for the operator to change them in their favor later since they will be in the driver's seat at some point.
- **Carefully choose the deals you send over**: Make sure you thoroughly understand their geographic and size limitations and then only send deals that are a fit. And when you send the deal, don't just forward what you received from LoopNet, the seller, or a broker. Add your own analysis, valuation, photos, etc. Go beneath the facts and look for seller motivations, local demographic trends or news, and your own opinion on the pros and cons of the deal. Once you have some experience at this, you can even come up with your own maximum offer.
- **Plan to get an LOI and a draft contract**: Many operators will be impressed if you bring them an executed LOI and a draft contract. You may even want to do what I've done, which is to have a fully executed contract that is assignable to another party.
- **Don't take a commission**: If you are not a licensed real estate broker, it is illegal to perform the list of activities that only a broker

can do. And it is illegal to receive a commission. In my view, this is not the best way to progress down this path anyway. I am recommending the possibility that you stay involved in the acquisition and operation of the asset to learn the business and to earn a place at the table in the company and the industry.

- **Use this as a learning opportunity**: As part of the deal, ask the syndicator to include you in the whole process. Analysis, due diligence, the closing process, lending, cursory asset management, and a hundred other details provide a great opportunity for you to learn more about the business and prepare to do your own deals.
- **Get it on your resume**: I know a deal finder who has done this for a third-party buyer for 24 years. He has been credited by buyers and brokers as a key player, so he gets access to many deals that never hit the market. If he chooses to do his own deal, he has quite an impressive resume as part of several hundred million dollars in acquisitions over the past couple decades. Even if you don't want to be a syndicator/operator yourself, if you have access to deals, you could make a career of this. Your track record would be a great credibility boost when you speak to brokers, lenders, and investors in future years.

Two Examples

I've already shared two brief stories of my own. I love this path, and I think you'll love these true tales from the trenches.

More Than He Bargained for

I met Denny at a networking event many years ago. He was a tall emergency room doctor. He was probably in his late 30s, but he looked much older. He looked tired. And he was.

Denny told me his job was driving him crazy. He was working long shifts in an urban Southern California hospital that spit out staff with regularity. He said he couldn't last much longer there, and he was starting on a path to be a commercial real estate syndicator. We were both in a coaching program, and his goal was to get into the business as a deal finder. And he was going after it with passion.

I stayed in touch with Dennis to follow his progress. He did a careful city selection to determine where he wanted to invest. Then he used every spare hour to connect with brokers, contact sellers, and to take due diligence trips from Los Angeles, California, to two cities in Texas. His schedule allowed him to work a lot of hours at once then have several days off to chase his real estate dream.

I doubt that he could have gotten much traction with brokers as a newbie. Commercial brokers typically only pay attention to those who can put cash in their bank account. It helped that he was a doctor, but what helped more was the support he got from the coach, who took great interest in Denny's activities. They backed his efforts by following up with brokers and making offers on deals Denny turned over.

Pretty soon those offers turned into deals, and Denny got a slice of each one. Denny was making acquisition fees, building equity, gaining credibility, and learning the business at the same time. But he had to work hard to make this happen.

Denny was eventually able to replace his income and made plans to break free from the medical grind. But Denny got a welcome surprise. His coach and now syndication partner on several deals had been deeply impressed with his performance over these few years. It's hard to imagine how Denny's hard work could have paid off more!

"Why Are We Working to Make Our Bosses Rich?"

William and Patrick were longtime friends. They both worked in commercial real estate for about two decades. Their jobs were to locate land for a national commercial developer, and they were good at it. But they were working hard and not getting any younger.

One evening, at the end of another long, exhausting trip, they asked each other: "Why are we giving the best years of our lives to make our company owners rich? Why are we spending this much time away from our families to line others' pockets? Sure, our pay is nice, but we aren't building true wealth. No equity to pass on to our wives or kids." But they went back to work the next week and started all over.

It was about that time one of them was diagnosed with cancer. That was the spark that lit the flame. Like Dr. Denny, they joined a mentor program to learn how to syndicate their own deals. After a year in the program, they established their own company and were determined to find opportunities. Their coach agreed to partner with them, but he warned them that they must adhere to the firm's strict acquisition guidelines. This was nothing new to them since they'd lived with strict land procurement guidelines for 20 years.

After quite a few unsuccessful bids, they located a facility that was a perfect fit for their coach. They joined the coach to tour the property, calculate a value and bid, make an offer, place the facility under LOI then contract, and eventually close. They got a healthy chunk of the acquisition fee, a nice piece of ownership, and a deal in their name, which translated to credibility with brokers when they went to look for their second deal.

William and Patrick found their second successful deal in a nearby city, and they brought it to their syndication partner like before. This time they started to feel a familiar feeling. "Do we want to continue doing a lot of this upfront work to get a small slice of the pie... when we could buy and operate these deals ourselves?"

They realized the missing ingredient was getting passive investors. But they had been involved in almost every other aspect of these two deals, and they were confident they could pull this off too. And they did. William and Patrick did a few small commercial deals and then went on to launch their first commercial real estate fund. A fund like this can offer strong diversification across asset types, asset sizes, geographies, property managers, and time. Time refers to the fact that some assets are acquired later than others, and this can provide balance to a portfolio in an ever-changing economy.

One Brief Warning

This might be the most appealing path for many of you who can only dedicate part time effort to self-storage investing, or those of you who want to move quickly and make a profit within months. I get it. But I should tell you that, like all good things in life, this is not an easy path. It is certainly doable, but you will be competing against a small army of brokers and syndicators who want to acquire the same deals. Your challenge will be to find the deals and to connect with the owners that they don't.

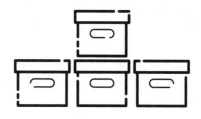

CHAPTER 12

PATH 4: BECOME A CAPITAL DEVELOPMENT SPECIALIST

Maybe you don't want to take the long and winding road to the top of the commercial self-storage mountain or the steep climb up the rock face of going it alone. Maybe you don't have access to off-market deals or brokers. But you do have access to cash—or at least people who have it.

If this describes you, you may be poised to travel one of the most lucrative paths of all: the path of the capital development specialist, who is a money-raiser and an equity-placement professional. It's been said that capital development is the most prized of all business skills. All businesses need capital, and all types of organizations need funding. Commercial and residential real estate deals, tech start-ups, and world-changing non-profits all have one thing in common—the need for capital.

You May Be Ideally Suited for This Path if You...

- Connect well with people.
- Have a circle of wealthy or well-connected friends.
- Are a good storyteller.
- Have natural sales skills or can learn them.
- Are willing to trust someone else to control the deal while you provide the money .
- Have the inclination to maintain relationships over time, through thick and thin.
- Can write, blog, speak, and do podcasts about what you're raising money for.

How Does This Work?

Please understand that I am not a legal professional, and this path requires significant legal guidance. There are SEC guidelines that govern this arena, and you need to find out for yourself how they may apply to your situation. Because these guidelines change over time and are sometimes based on case law, I'm encouraging you to investigate on your own before proceeding on Path 4.

In a commercial real estate partnership, it is likely that responsibilities will be divided. Perhaps one partner is responsible for finding and analyzing deals, another for operations and asset management, and a third for raising capital and maintaining ongoing investor relations.

Though you may not have the skills and track record to pull off the first two roles at this stage in your career, perhaps you are in a position to fill the role of capital raiser right now, and this could be your entry point into a commercial real estate partnership. Note that I talk in terms of partnership for this path, because SEC guidelines state that this role cannot be relegated to an unlicensed employee or contractor. (I'm referring to a broker-dealer license for financial professionals.) You must be a legitimate partner in a deal to talk to investors about investing, or you need to be licensed, which is an entirely different matter.

How Do You Find an Operator?

You may already be aware of an operator whom you'd like to raise capital for or a syndicator who is recruiting equity partners for their next deal.

If not, don't despair. As I said, capital development is perhaps the most valuable business skill, and you can find someone else in need of the equity you can bring.

There is a broad and growing network of self-storage and other commercial real estate syndicators that you can tap into. These operators may be found in mastermind groups, on podcasts, on investing forums such as BiggerPockets, and in your own city's Real Estate Investors Association (REIA).

Do yourself a favor and be careful who you partner with. Realize that as the go-between for investors, the operator, and their deal, you are signing yourself up for trouble. Nothing ever goes exactly as planned. Investors will be expecting you to underpromise and overdeliver. Realize that you will be the face of that operator to them—you represent that deal to them. Yet you will have virtually no control over the success or failure of that deal. Basically, you will have virtually no say in the operation or its results.

When you sign up to be such a partner, you need to ask yourself, "Do I like and trust this operator enough to be in an intimate relationship with them for the next decade or so? Do I want to put my name on the line to represent them and endure the ups and downs and current unknowns that will come our way? Is this operator and this deal well positioned with a margin of safety to endure the eventual downturn that will occur as part of every normal economic cycle?" etc.

What Should You Look for in an Operator/Partner?

I am managing director for three funds that invest in commercial real estate deals. Self-storage is one of our favorite assets, and when we invest in a deal, we start by looking carefully at the operator. I suggest you do a similar deep dive on a syndicator/operator before ever considering one of their deals. Before looking at an operator, you should examine what type of strategy you want to pursue. You may be looking for:

- a ground-up development;
- a steep value-add;
- a mom-and-pop to buy, upgrade, and sell to a REIT (my favorite);
- a stabilized cash-flowing deal; or
- any of the above with a long-term hold (refinancing out excess "lazy" equity along the way).

Mindset

While it can be a good idea to narrow down which strategy you're look-ing for, I recommend that you be open-minded at this point. You may change your mind once you find a trusted operator who has a strategy that has produced proven results and is better than the one you had planned to pursue.

You may also have a certain geography in mind. Again, I would recommend that you prioritize finding the right operator and trusting them to find the best geographies. Then you can follow the well-known adage: Trust but verify.

This is what I love about this mindset and way of entering the busi-ness: You don't have to be the expert. You can parlay your skills and circle of influence into an expert's company and track record without going through the years of pain to build a company from the ground up.

Our real estate fund looks for operators with a long list of important qualities. We look for operators who:

- share our conservative investment mindset;
- have survived or thrived through one or more recessions and know how to navigate a downturn;
- have built an experienced team that knows how to convert a mom-and-pop facility to a stabilized asset that could be acquired by an institutional investor (or profitably held long term);
- have relationships with brokers and sellers that result in a steady stream of off-market acquisition opportunities;
- have often focused more on operations than on raising capital and could benefit from the equity we can infuse;
- have a track record of selling stabilized assets to REITs and other institutional buyers for a significant profit; and
- have offered us a significantly better deal based on our economies of scale (bringing them a large check).

On that last point, I mean that we like to work with operators who are willing to give our funds (our investors) a preferred ROI based on the fact that we are bringing one large check. We often bring about $1 million to an individual deal, which represents about 13 or 14 accredited investors averaging about $75,000 each. This is a group of investors that we have a relationship with and that the syndicator/operator will never have to meet or service.

This is just a shortened version of our list, and I encourage you to come up with your own. Feel free to start with ours and add your own criteria.

How Much Can You Make?

As I mentioned, you cannot make a commission doing this unless you are a licensed FINRA representative, working under a registered broker dealer. FINRA stands for Financial Industry Regulatory Authority. FINRA is a government-authorized nonprofit that oversees U.S. broker-dealers. You may be able to get a flat introduction or referral fee per investor, but it is *critical* that the fee not be based on how much the investor invests in the current deal or any future deals. A typical introduction fee for accredited investors is on the order of $1,000 to $2,000 but can vary widely. Some attorneys believe that even this fee is questionable.

I am suggesting a longer-term relationship with a syndicator/operator. I am suggesting that you really get to know them on a deep level and create such value for them that they invite you to be a general partner in one (or more) of their deals. This may not be as hard as you think. As I said, raising equity is a valuable skill and could be in high demand. There are great operators out there who love to acquire and operate but don't like to raise capital. I already told you about one who retrofit a Kmart last year and stands to make a large return on his equity over a three-year project. He has little interest in raising capital. You would have done well raising the equity for that deal.

Other Benefits of This Path

Some would-be syndicators take this path for goals that transcend income. It could be a great opportunity to learn the syndicated commercial real estate business. You would have the chance to shadow more experienced owner-operators and hopefully learn to do this for yourself. Or you could choose to stay in the role of capital raiser for this operator or others—and laser focus is not a bad thing.

You may be able to add the deal to your resume. Being an integral part of the general partnership is something you can add to your qualifications for the day when you talk to brokers, sellers, lenders, and investors to start doing your own deals. This is extremely valuable, as I mentioned in chapter 5 about barriers to entry.

You will also form many new relationships along the way. By being an A player, you will make yourself a critical member to the team, and you will get noticed inside and outside the organization. I would hope that the other partners come to see you as a crucial part of the group and therefore give you a larger stake in future deals.

Licensure: One More Option on This Path

Though I don't think many of you will use this option, some of you may want to consider licensure. This is the SEC's preferred path for those who are not principals in their own deals.

You may elect to become a registered representative. This will mean working under a broker dealer and being regulated by FINRA, but it will allow you to charge a commission for raising capital. FINRA guidelines will result in a lot of restrictions on advertising, blogging, podcasting, and more.

You may also become a registered investment advisor (RIA). Though this avenue doesn't allow you to charge commissions in the same way as those working under a broker dealer, I understand that RIAs often have a lot more freedom in their activities. They are compensated based on a percentage of the assets they have under management or on an hourly basis.

I've limited my comments here because this is an area I don't know much about. But I wanted you to be aware that this is an option if you pursue the capital-raising path. Note that it may be a bad idea to become FINRA registered and then try to partner with a real estate syndicator later. The restrictions imposed by FINRA might carry over to the future (even if you ditch your license). You need to weigh the pros and cons carefully before pursuing this option.

A Final Thought

If you plan to raise capital for your own deals or others', education is a great place to start. You won't go wrong by reading Matt Faircloth's excellent book *Raising Private Capital: Building Your Real Estate Empire Using Other People's Money* (BiggerPockets Publishing, 2018).

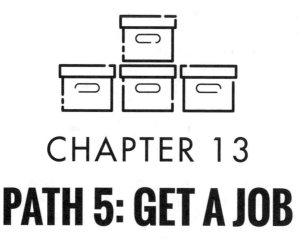

CHAPTER 13
PATH 5: GET A JOB

For certain people, and in certain seasons, it makes the most sense to start down the path toward real estate world domination by getting a job. Yes, I'm talking about one with a good old W-2 paycheck—a path that most baby boomers and prior generations saw as the only option, but one that seems increasingly scorned.

Consider that many of the great real estate investors of our day started off on this path. Take my friend Andrew, for example. Andrew got out of college and worked his way through the ranks at Equity Residential, the third-largest commercial multifamily operator in the United States. He spent 10 years honing his operational skills and was in charge of a $2.5 billion portfolio for the last five years of his time with this company. During his tenure, he was instrumental in the acquisition of over 30 new assets totaling $3.5 billion and the disposition of 20 properties totaling $285 million in sales.

After a decade with this REIT, Andrew decided to move to a private owner to broaden his experience and understanding of the business. He took the role of senior director of operations for the largest privately held multifamily owner in the United States. He led a team of regional managers who oversaw a portfolio of 9,215 units in nine states across the Mid-Atlantic, Southeast, Midwest, and Southwest. During his time there, he was instrumental in the architecture of this company, which had exponential growth but required a significant upgrade in its structure and policies to continue on that path.

Andrew was traveling three weeks out of the month. With a desire to get off the road, Andrew left to take a position with a large local family office to oversee their commercial and multifamily assets. (A *family office* is the business and investment management office for a wealthy family.) Andrew's days were spent handling five multifamily assets, 150,000 square feet of retail space, two 600-space garages, a 90-acre mixed-use development project, and a $40 million high-rise redevelopment on Biscayne Bay in the neighborhood South Beach of Miami, Florida.

About that time, a growing company in Richmond, Virginia, was looking for someone to take over asset management for its portfolio. Andrew's resume came to the heads of the company, and the breadth of his experience plus the cultural fit were a perfect match. He made the move four years ago. In contrast to his previous positions, Andrew now gets a stake in each of the deals he manages. This equity piece is something that Andrew never received in his previous jobs. Now he can personally benefit from the success of the properties he helps guide.

You May Be Ideally Suited for This Path if You...

- Are already working in one of these fields, or have a connection that works for a company in these fields.
- Are a college student and undecided about your major—considering real estate for your degree will be a great stepping stone.
- Are okay with gaining experience first and achieving wealth later.
- Feel like you need to work full time to sustain your livelihood, while gaining knowledge about the commercial investment space.
- Are driven, hard-working, and love to hustle.

What Are the Ideal Jobs on This Path?

1. Property manager
2. Asset manager
3. Financial analyst

4. Commercial real estate broker

5. Commercial real estate lender

While there may be other occupations that will put you on the path, I think these five will cover most of the bases.

Property Manager

Many self-storage syndication firms manage their own facilities. Others use third-party management firms, which employ a variety of staff, including frontline managers, regional managers, accountants, and more. By taking a job as a self-storage property manager, you will learn the detailed ins and outs of this business from the ground up. You will learn all about:

- Marketing
- Sales
- Customer service
- Pricing
- Maintenance and repair
- Capital projects
- Grounds
- Inventory (POS items, etc.)
- Bookkeeping
- Legal (evictions, auctions, etc.)

There are other benefits to this job:

- You will get to know and prove yourself to middle and senior management.
- You will learn about competitors and others in the business.
- You will attend industry trade shows and business events in your community.
- You should get significant training and education.
- You may have the chance to work your way up to regional or senior management over time.

Real estate investing has skyrocketed in popularity, and many entrepreneurs have entered in this space. However, surprisingly few in commercial real estate have done the hard work to learn their business from the ground up. This path could give you an advantage over many.

Asset Manager

Who manages the property managers? Who is responsible, on behalf of the owners and their investors, for ensuring that the property managers are doing all they can, and that the assets are meeting the financial objectives that were outlined at purchase? That is the role of the asset manager.

The property management firm, which is often a contracted third party, needs to be held accountable for the budget and a thousand other things. Because property managers often work for another firm, or at least another boss, their loyalties can be divided. They may find themselves having to do what is best for one party at the expense of another.

The asset manager is an integral part of the syndicator's/owner's team, and their role is to serve as a manager of the property managers and the properties. Their job is to ensure that everyone is pulling in the same direction and doing whatever is possible to maximize income and value on behalf of the owners and their investors. At a large commercial real estate firm, the asset management team may have roles that you could fill.

This could be a great way to learn what property managers do while working directly on behalf of the owners and investors. It could also be a way to meet key leaders in the company or the industry and to prove yourself to them and their peers. By making yourself valuable to them, you may earn a promotion, or you may meet peers who invite you to join them to start a new partnership. This is certainly an option worth considering for many.

Financial Analyst

Are you a wiz with spreadsheets? Do you love numbers and thrive on financial ratios? There's a lot of number crunching involved in both the acquisition and the ongoing management of commercial self-storage facilities, and many of those with the cash don't have the time or inclination to do all that number crunching on their own. They may understand the numbers but not be as familiar with the latest software or management tools, or they just don't have the time to keep up with all of the formulas and spreadsheets to optimally analyze and manage properties.

If you have the inclination and the skills, you may find your way into the commercial real estate realm as a financial analyst. I suggest you look for opportunities with a larger firm or with a firm that you already have some connection to. Most entrepreneurial firms won't have a paid position like this for you, but you may even want to volunteer to do this type of work for a smaller firm. Make yourself irreplaceable and you could land a job, and that could lead to a career or your own ownership stake at some point.

One of the partners in my firm started out as a financial analyst with us during his senior year in college. He proved himself in this role and significantly supported us in the asset management arena as well. Now in his mid-20s, he has a significant ownership stake in our firm and is positioned to grow at the company over the coming decades.

Commercial Real Estate Broker

A great commercial real estate broker is worth their weight in gold to self-storage operators and their investors. Some generalist commercial real estate brokerage firms have brokers who specialize in brokering self-storage deals. Other generalist firms have brokers who perform all types of commercial transactions. Still other firms engage specifically in self-storage brokerage.

If you want to go down this path to become a self-storage master, I recommend that you specialize in self-storage brokerage. I've met only a handful of agents who do this well, and you could become one of them. By taking this path, you will learn the industry. You will meet all the players, from mom-and-pop owners to REITs. You will learn how to do a deep dive into the financials because you will have to prepare them for listing proposals and marketing packages. You will get to know lenders and even some investors. And you will have the advantage of not having to punch a clock.

Unlike an asset manager or a financial analyst, as a commercial real estate broker you would likely be an independent contractor who is paid on a commission-only basis. As such, you'll probably get to set your own hours and determine your own pay and destiny.

Though it may be tempting, I recommend you not take financial positions in the deals you broker. I know of one commercial broker who started investing in their own deals and now has a shady reputation in the investment community. That is not to say that you couldn't make a break with your commercial brokerage at some point and become a syndicator. I think that would be a promising option.

Commercial Real Estate Lender

A key component to multiplying your wealth in commercial real estate investing is safe debt. Leverage can produce a great ROI and allow an increase in value to become an exponential increase in your wealth. A reliable lender is a key player in this scenario, which is why I recommend taking a job as a commercial lender.

As a member of the lending team, you will meet a lot of real estate syndicators and get to know them quite well. You will also meet some investors and get to know the staff at family offices and private equity firms. Find opportunities to make site visits, underwrite deals, and truly climb inside the heads of buyers and sellers of commercial real estate. You will learn about marketing as you market your own services. Oh, and you also may make a lot of money.

This option and the previous one (real estate broker) are the two routes that are the most entrepreneurial—and either may result in feast or famine. Both are compensated through commission, and I can imagine that if you do well in one of these roles, you may decide to stay on this path for a long time. Perhaps permanently.

I can imagine the commercial lender subpath, more than the broker subpath, being done in conjunction with some of the other major paths I discuss in this section of the book. You could be a lender and invest passively too. I know someone who does this successfully. It is possible to be a deal finder on the side, and I think you could be a capital raiser as well. I also know of a prominent commercial lender who parlayed his contacts and experience into becoming a successful syndicator. He now owns over 7,000 units, mostly in the Dallas area.

What Are Some of the Challenges to Expect on This Path?

Getting paid while you learn and make valuable connections from within profitable companies can be great, but there are potential challenges too. First of all, many of the companies that can afford to pay you a salary are probably more corporate rather than entrepreneurial, and you might not get exactly the types of opportunities you want on the inside. On the other hand, the more entrepreneurial companies might not have positions for you. This is a generalization, of course.

It is possible that during your tenure you will meet a like-minded person with whom you can partner to leverage what you've learned and start a new venture. That is how many of the greatest companies have been born, as history has repeatedly shown.

There's also the salary and benefits trap. You may get so comfortable with your paycheck, benefits, and predictable hours that you won't want to leave, especially if your life gets more complicated with a spouse, a mortgage, and additional mouths to feed. There's nothing wrong with this, but just be aware that it may not lead you to your goal.

As I mentioned earlier, there is the potential for conflict of interest. Any time your long-term goal is not aligned with your current role, there's a chance that you could find yourself acting in your own best interests on your employer's dime. This can be a slippery slope, especially in an age when notifications are coming at you on multiple devices in your workplace, home, and car. Sometimes it's hard to draw the line between work and your personal time and efforts, and though you may feel that you are doing everything right, your employer may see things differently.

QUICK INSIGHTS

The World's Most Famous Real Estate Broker

It's not hard to guess his name. He took his brokerage from a local Austin, Texas, office to a regional player to North America's largest network of brokerages in a relatively short time.

You may not know the names of many brokerage founders and leaders, but if you've been involved in real estate for any time at all, you know of the co-founder of Keller Williams.

Were you aware that Gary Keller started his career by studying real estate in college? At a time when college degrees in real estate were virtually unheard of, Gary went to Baylor University in Waco, Texas, to obtain a degree in real estate and insurance.

After getting his degree, he relocated to Austin, where he joined a firm and sold five houses in his first month. He made it his goal to rise to vice president, which he did a little over four years later—right before he left to launch a competitor.

Keller joined with Joe Williams to start a pair of brokerage firms on both the residential and commercial side. Keller's unique win-win mindset; his focus on God, family, and business; and his intense training, education, and generous ownership model propelled the rapid growth of the firm. The rest is history.

What's my point? If you are still undecided about your future and plan to go to college (Keller almost didn't), you may want to consider a degree in real estate. I know quite a few investors who are currently pursuing this path, and regardless of which path you pursue after graduation, this may be a good starting point.

How Do You Get Started on This Path?

There is no precise formula, but I'm happy to offer a few suggestions. First, I would make a list of all your contacts and figure out which ones may have leads on the route you hope to take. This may mean attending a local real estate meetup or REIA and asking around. It may include asking those on your list who they know so you can build your network.

Then I would review job postings—locally first, but perhaps regionally and nationally as well. There are so many online job sources that I won't bother to list them. You may want to select a company you'd like to work for and connect with HR or someone else inside the firm to see if you can get leads that aren't posted publicly.

You can also approach firms with your resume and a cover letter. Are you willing to serve in an apprentice role in order to get coaching and a foot in the door? Great. Say that succinctly, in a one-page proposal. If you are given a small task or two to accomplish, do them extremely well, exceeding the standards and expectations of the boss. Many do this on a limited basis, such as one day per week or during off-hours. Others have a spouse who can fund them doing more. I cover this idea in more detail in Path 7.

And don't forget to check the BiggerPockets forums and network. BiggerPockets is the world's largest network of real estate investors, and you may find local or regional connections there that you can't find elsewhere.

A Real-Life Example

I'm excited to share the unfolding story of my friend Joe Mascow. I met Joe at a self-storage mastermind a few years ago, and we stayed in touch. I was impressed with the bold, sacrificial steps he has taken to walk the path of ownership and wealth. Joe was a residential loan officer in his former career. He was making six-figures as a young man, and life was good. But he was working hard to earn his money, and he realized he didn't want to keep going at this pace forever. He wanted to create passive income, and he was just trading hours for dollars in the mortgage business.

At some point along the way, Joe heard about self-storage, and he realized that owning facilities of his own would be a great path for him to achieve true wealth. Rather than try to jump straight into an owner's role (he was in his late 20s), he decided to take the "get-a-job" path. It seemed most natural to pursue a position as a self-storage property manager.

Then he found out what property managers earn. It would be a 60 percent pay cut from his comfortable commission as a mortgage broker. But he viewed this like going to college, with its sacrifices of time and money. Joe had a vision for the long term over short term gains, and I really admired him for that. His primary goal was to learn about the functions of an owner, so he looked for a job with the largest facility he could find. He was hired as the manager of a 1,000-unit self-storage facility north of Dallas. His salary was about $50,000.

About two years into his tenure there, I asked Joe to describe his experience. I was surprised when he quickly said, "It's sure not glamorous!"

He believes he actually made a mistake in taking on the management of a 1,000-unit facility right out of the gate. He said, "I might have learned more at a facility half this size. With a thousand units, I have to run hard for long hours every day just to keep up. I don't have the time to innovate and test new ideas. I don't have the opportunity to get out into the community to bolster our marketing efforts and get to know colleagues and competitors. That is the one thing I would do differently, but it would mean an even deeper pay cut."

Joe went on to emphasize the importance of learning to live on less than his income while he could, at his former pay, so he'd be able to live on less when he had to later, in his new role.

I asked Joe about his biggest wins in the process.

He said, "I kept a journal, and I'm so glad I did. I was able to maintain a record of lessons I learned, and this enables me to look back now and remember what it was like to be ignorant of so much I take for granted now, a few years later. This will help me guide property managers working at my facility in the future. And it will help me know when they're trying to fool me."

Joe also keeps a record of tangible progress and mistakes. This is for his own journal as well as to report to the owner about how his actions have led to a more profitable and valuable self-storage asset. And to candidly disclose where he could have done better.

Joe also makes a practice of listening carefully to tenant suggestions and complaints. He takes notes in their presence to show them he genuinely cares about their concerns and ideas to make the facility better. Of course, he can't implement all of them, but when he does, he takes the effort to reach out to the tenant to tell them how he responded to their request. This requires diligent follow-through, which is a trait of a great employee and a great owner.

When I asked Joe to summarize his experience as a property manager, he said the benefits of this path were more valuable than he had originally imagined. And like anything good in life, they came with a higher price tag than he expected.

He recapped his experience as follows:

- I made great contacts in the industry, both locally and nationally;
- I met many of the most important vendors I would need when owning my own facility;
- I learned what works well versus poorly in marketing and operations;
- I learned to discern fact from fiction when getting reports from a subordinate employee;
- I gained credibility with staff, real estate brokers, lenders, and owners;
- I have first-hand knowledge of pricing, supply and demand, and how to configure unit mixes;
- I have real experience in understanding how a new competitor in the market can hurt sales;
- I know how to make customers happy, and I also know what they don't really care about;
- I understand what policies and procedures are important versus those that are frivolous;
- I've discovered what I'll need to do myself as an owner someday versus what can be hired out or delegated;
- I have a better idea of what to look for in a self-storage asset to acquire, and;
- I know how to locate and hire a great property manager for my own self-storage facility when the time is right.

I've always counseled people to take more risks at a young age. Joe doesn't have an onerous mortgage payment or a wife and kids to support.

He is perfectly positioned to make this sacrifice now, and I expect he will be glad he did for decades to come.

What about you? Are you willing to delay your investment or ownership goals to learn the business from the ground-up as a property manager, lender, commercial broker, analyst, or asset manager? This may be a path of financial and time sacrifice today that could launch you into a brilliant future tomorrow. Many of you are not in a position to tread this path. For those of you who are, however, I recommend you seriously consider it.

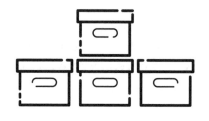

CHAPTER 14

PATH 6: TAKE THE PASSIVE PATH

The cry of the passive investor: "Why work harder than I need to, to make less than I could?"

As a content provider for BiggerPockets, as well as a fund manager, I have the privilege of interacting with hundreds of single-family and small multifamily real estate investors every year. Many are trying to do one flip at a time. Others are trying to build a portfolio to replace their income. I've found that most of them eventually come to the same conclusion, although I hear them voice it in different ways. They say:

"What am I doing? I'm looking for a few flip and rental homes, and I'm beating my head against a wall every spare moment—and getting nowhere!"

"I had a goal to build a portfolio of several dozen rentals to retire on. I am up to four now, and I'm pulling my hair out. This doesn't seem sustainable."

"I've reached the goal I thought I wanted. I have over a hundred single-family and small multifamily units. But the economies of scale aren't there. This is driving me crazy, and I can't keep this up another year, far less several decades. I want out!"

Recently, I was talking to a highly successful single-family and small multifamily owner/operator. He's relatively young, and he's amassed about 325 units in North Dakota ranging from single-family homes to small multifamily properties and even a few mobile home parks. He's a smart guy who has broken through the barrier into the big time. He has a management team in place, and he's achieved what most single-family investors only dream of.

But he called me because he is searching for a way out. He said he's tired of the 70-hour weeks. He has two small kids and is not living the life he expected to at this point, so he's looking to sell off two-thirds of his portfolio and go passive.

If any of this resonates with you, you may want to reconsider your plans. It may be best for you to follow the path outlined in this chapter by marshalling your cash, vetting a fantastic operator, and investing passively with them. You may find yourself enjoying life, making more money, saving more on taxes, and not experiencing the crushing pain of failure that comes along the path of most start-ups. By joining a seasoned syndicator *after* the pain of their failures, you may be able to avoid those losses and share in their profits and appreciation.

You May Be Ideally Suited for This Path if You...

- Have more liquid capital than you have time and experience.
- Are stewarding a significant sum of money from friends or family.
- Like the returns and tax shield provided by commercial real estate but don't want to be a sponsor/operator.
- Think the timing isn't right for you to become a full-time sponsor/operator just yet.
- Have found a sponsor you trust who will allow you to look over their shoulder.
- Don't want the burden of acquiring a large self-storage asset as a part-time endeavor but are fine with watching how others do it while you stay at your job or enjoy retirement.

Three Passive Investment Subpaths

Subpath 1: Truly Passive Investor

On this passive path variation, you find a syndicator or sponsor/operator you trust and send them a check. Finding someone you trust is the main goal. Then you count on them to choose the asset class, geography, and deal that make the most sense. This should be an operator with a boat-load of experience, a great track record, glowing references, gleaming background checks, and more.

Subpath 2: Professional Passive Investor

Although similar to the subpath previously mentioned, this one involves not just choosing a syndicator and trusting them to do all the right deals, but also carefully evaluating each individual deal.

Therefore, this subpath requires a lot more involvement on your part. You will need to get to know the demographic and geographic issues that are important to you, understand the numbers and be able to critically evaluate a proforma, learn to ask hard questions, and travel to each location to see it for yourself.

I know of investors who trust a certain syndicator and simply invest in each deal they do. I know of others who love a particular syndicator but evaluate each deal critically, saying yes to some and no to others. Either path is fine, but the latter will be more time-consuming. The upside is you may get better results.

Subpath 3: Passive Crowdfunding Investor

The JOBS Act of 2012 opened up a wide variety of crowdfunding investment opportunities to many who may have found it difficult to invest before. Hundreds of crowdfunding platforms sprang up around the web, and investors went from too few opportunities to perhaps too many to choose from.

You might assume that these crowdfunding sites carefully vet all the syndicators on their platform. While they seem to do a pretty good job with some basic hurdles, I don't believe they always perform the level of due diligence that you would want when selecting a syndicator. Keep in mind that they generally make money on the transaction, not on the performance of each investment.

With that in mind, I recommend you visit the platforms to gather information. Listen to the pitches and read through the details. Meet a number of sponsors, ask hard questions, and get to know them. But before you invest, be sure to perform the same level of due diligence you would for any other deal. Ignore the fact that you found the syndicator on a crowdfunding platform. Make the trips. Meet them in person. Check their backgrounds and references. Drive to the site and review the comps.

The only exception I would make is in the event that you are investing a very small, "insignificant" amount of your capital. While I hate to see any money unnecessarily at risk, if you want to test a sponsor out for a future larger investment and they offer a low minimum, perhaps you could invest without performing such rigorous due diligence.

Vetting a Partner and a Deal

Because of the importance of partnering with the right sponsor, I'm going to devote some time to the vetting process. Even if you are taking one of the other paths, please consider these guidelines as you vet your operating partner.

1. **Be active before becoming passive**: There will come a day when you write a check, send it off, then sit back and relax, waiting for the monthly or quarterly distribution. But to really be able to relax and enjoy this process for years to come, you'll need to be a hound dog first. Before sending a five- or six-figure check to anyone, you must get to know them. Please don't take this lightly. You will be financially married to this operator for years or decades to come, and this covenant should be entered into with all the due diligence you are able to muster.

2. **Perform a background check**: More than at any time in history, we now have almost unlimited access to information on people and companies. Take the time and spend the money to learn everything you can about a syndicator. Check out their social media pages. Do searches with their name and "SEC violation" together. Add state names to the search. Pay for a background check, and don't be shy about asking the syndicator about the results. (Note that these can contain errors, so you should give syndicators a chance to defend themselves if something looks amiss. I once received a report containing a spousal abuse charge, but it turned out to refer to a different person with the same name.)

3. **Ask for references**: Check them carefully. Ask hard questions, and if possible, find references the syndicator did not offer. Of course, you should ask all of them, "Would you invest with ___ again?" And since one of the major passive investor frustrations is lack of communication, be sure to ask the sponsor (also known as the syndicator) and their references about this issue.

4. **Review the private placement memorandum (PPM)**: Each syndication will provide a PPM for your review. This is a lengthy document that few people actually read. Do yourself a favor and read it. It includes details on the syndicator's history and track record plus a lengthy list of risks for the project you are considering. Although the risk factors were compiled by an experienced attorney, they can be real and should not be shrugged off. Schedule a follow-up call with the sponsor to ask hard questions about the details of the PPM.

5. **Apply the scuttlebutt method**: Phil Fisher explains this method in his renowned book *Common Stocks and Uncommon Profits*. You need to get to the unofficial story (the scuttlebutt) from those closest to the project and the sponsor. That may mean showing up on-site to review the project and the competing assets, and having a friendly conversation with the sponsor's administrative assistant to see how they are really treated. It could mean meeting with the sponsor for lunch and observing how they treat the server or the Uber driver. Speak to the accountant. Talk to the tenants. Find out how they treat other investors. Take your due diligence to a new level, and if you approach the syndicator with a concern and they bristle, it's time to find a new one. Don't ever accept "Don't worry. We've got that covered" as a syndicator's reply to a concern you voice.

Several months ago, we were considering an investment in a deal several states away. We had already vetted the operator and gone through many of the steps discussed here. On a visit to the site, I grilled everyone I could talk to. I learned that there were two new self-storage facilities under construction just a few miles away. These had not been reported in the competitive analysis, and it turned out the sponsor was unaware of them. We didn't invest in that deal.

Another time, I was evaluating a sponsor and continually dogged him with questions about a drainage easement along the edge of the proposed development. "Are you sure this won't cause a flood risk?" I didn't like his answers. It turned out that his construction team had dealt with the issue, and it was going to be fine. But apparently, I had irritated the guy to the point that he became unresponsive to me later. Though we liked the deal, we were happy to move on to invest with someone else.

6. **Examine the loan terms**: Don't skip over this. What is the interest rate? Is it locked in or can it fluctuate? What are the LTV ratio and the DSCR? When does the loan mature? What is the break-even occupancy on the deal?

7. **Scrutinize the proforma**: If you're traveling along subpath 2, you will definitely want to learn how to read proforma (projected) financial statements. You should get to know generally acceptable ranges for operating costs, lease-up assumptions, revenue increases, other income, and more. Take a close look at the operator's fees. Are their property management fees reasonable? What about their acquisition fees? Are they charging an ongoing asset management fee, and if so, is it contingent on performance? What about a fee at refinance or disposition?

8. **Review alignment and splits**: Do whatever you can to confirm that the syndicator's interests are aligned with yours. You don't want to be in a deal that benefits the syndicator but hurts you, or vice versa. How is the profit and ownership split calculated? Is there a preferred return? What is the split above the return?

9. **Ask other hard questions**: Don't be shy. Ask anything you think will help you make the right decision. That might include asking for a copy of the lease agreement the syndicator uses for tenants. Review their business plan. Ask for a detailed explanation of their worst deal and how they handled it.

10. **Start small**: One way to mitigate risk is to invest at the minimum level. Though you may have a large chunk of cash to allocate and feel comfortable that you've carefully vetted a great syndicator, you would probably be better off splitting up that cash among several asset classes, operators, and deals. Yes, this is a lot more work for you. But it's likely that at least one of them will shine brightly above the others. By holding back some of your capital, you will be able to benefit by diversifying. You can then place more funds with the operators who are initially performing best.

11. **Get *The Hands-Off Investor* (BiggerPockets Publishing, 2020)**: Syndicator and fund manager Brian Burke has written an excellent

guide for vetting commercial syndicators. Though his context is multifamily, his principles apply to self-storage and other commercial asset classes. Don't invest passively without reading this book.

What Are the Benefits of This Path?

Many investors realize the growth and income potential of commercial real estate, but they don't have the experience to acquire and operate assets on their own. This path provides a great opportunity to tap into decades of someone else's experience.

If you plan to invest in multiple deals, it is arguably easier to go through a single process to vet one or two great operators than it is to analyze every deal. If they are a great sponsor, they will do the heavy lifting on future analysis. If you're vetting hundreds of your own potential deals, you have no opportunity to model someone else.

As a passive investor, you will enjoy the income, appreciation, and tax benefits of this asset class. You stand to make sizable returns without quitting your day job or interrupting your retirement. Yes, you may leave a little money on the table, but you're likely to gain more profit by investing with experts. You will forgo control but also forgo a lot of hassle and risk. You may lose the thrill of the hunt, but you'll free up opportunities to find your thrills elsewhere.

What Challenges Should You Expect Along This Path?

Do you love control? You won't have it on this path. You are essentially trusting someone else with your capital and believing that they will do a better job than you would. Additionally, while a syndicator earns a premium for their time and experience, you will not get this benefit. Passive investors are all treated the same in most cases.

Though I can't quantify this for you, I can state that you may not get the same thrill of victory as the one "in the arena of battle." I would also say that you're less likely to experience the outcome of the agony of defeat by taking the passive path. Investing alongside experienced syndicators is far more likely to turn out well than acquiring an asset and running it on your own. The history, the team, the systems, and the synergies brought to the table by these operators is hard to match on your own.

How Do You Get Started?

I would start down this path by learning to research sponsors. You can begin to gain access and practice by visiting various crowdfunding sites and taking deep dives into their offering memorandums, track records, PPMs, and more. Sign up for their webinars and take note of what other attendees are asking.

You can also team up with other passive investors you connect with at meetups, conferences, or REIA meetings. You may also want to get to know the ins and outs of crowdfunding. This growing investment vehicle can be a great way to learn more about a wide variety of passive real estate investment sponsors and opportunities in one place.

Many investors take a long trudge and experience several painful ups and downs, then wind up as passive real estate investors. This path often starts with a slog through single-family real estate or other paths. As I said before, many investors go through years of banging their heads against a wall only to come to the realization that they would be happier as passive investors.

It's not easy to do all the things necessary to run a business of any kind, and self-storage is no exception. A lot of people would be happier and wealthier by investing with someone else who knows the business well. If that describes you, one of the passive options is likely the best route for you.

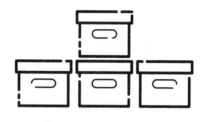

CHAPTER 15

PATH 7: FIND A COACH OR MENTOR

I recently started my third decade in real estate investing, and I am deeply involved on BiggerPockets and elsewhere. If there's one consistent question I get month in and month out, it's this: "Where can I find a mentor?"

I want to help. But more often than not, my answer comes up short. With the variety of asset types, investor experience levels and locations, as well as financial situations, it can be challenging to match up mentors and mentees. I think the lack of college education in the real estate field as well as the entrepreneurial nature of this business has fueled the fire for more and better mentoring programs.

I illuminate this final path with an overview of two types of mentoring scenarios plus a way to mentor yourself right into a self-storage ownership role. Then I close by telling one of my favorite mentoring success stories. I think you'll love this!

You May Be Ideally Suited for This Path if You...

- Are eager to jump-start your self-storage career but have no experience in this arena.
- Have the funds to pay a coach or mastermind group.
- Have savings (or income through a working spouse) to work full- or part-time for a mentor with little or no pay.
- Believe in the power of hiring a paid coach or mentor to help you move forward in your real estate career.

Two Types of Mentors and an Ownership Strategy

Mentors come in all shapes and styles—and at different prices—but I believe they generally fall into two categories. I'll explain these two then provide a unique strategy related to the mentor-apprentice relationship.

Paid Coaches

Paid coaching has skyrocketed in popularity in the past decade, for better and for worse. When I was first involved in real estate, as an investor and a broker, there were a limited number of coaching programs available. And many of them were of the guru variety.

Some of these programs consist of pre-recorded online webinars with some interaction and participation. They may offer a community of online support. Other programs consist of a weekend event that often gives the student valuable information and then offers them a chance to join an ongoing program or community for more training and support.

Some programs consist of a hefty upfront fee that pays for the entire program, which are especially popular these days. Some come with a small monthly payment along the way as well. These programs tend to foster a long-term relationship. This can lead to a partnership between the student and the coach, which can be a great opportunity for the student.

BiggerPockets has a stance against unethical gurus. Although I can't tell you how to always recognize them, other than if it sounds too good to be true, it probably is. If they're making big promises that appeal to your ego and your desire to make a lot of money with little effort, watch out. While not all paid coaches are money-hungry gurus, do a quick background check in the BiggerPockets forums by asking about a coaching program you're interested in before schilling out the cash.

Master-Apprentice Relationship

Have you read about the master-apprentice relationship? This was a wonderful opportunity to learn a trade in prior centuries. Though not as widely known now, this process can still work today.

My son, Jonathon, a successful real estate investor, has done two internships with mentors who worked in this fashion. Though these relationships often lasted for seven years in centuries past, my son did a one-year program for his first one, and his second one lasted about two years. Then he went to college to study the same subject. His determination and experience in the field put him at the top of his class and helped him launch a profitable career. This took some time and willpower, as well as a few years with limited income, but it paid off in a big way.

Though these relationships are hard to find, they can be great avenues to teach you about real estate investing, property management, syndication, and more. If you have the time and willingness to submit yourself to this process, you can start by approaching a successful real estate investor—say a self-storage owner or syndicator—to request mentoring in their trade.

But be careful how you approach them. If you go saying, "Please teach me your trade," you'll scare them away. This sounds like a time drain with no benefit for them. It's better for you to offer them your skills first. Find out what they need. It could be work as a webmaster, an online marketing person, a copywriter, a financial analyst, someone to work the phones to find deals, or good old grunt work. Then if relevant, tell them about your applicable skills and how you would be willing to assist them. And tell them that in exchange you'd like to shadow them to learn the business.

Don't be surprised if they're doubtful about your follow through. They probably get offers like this often. Make sure you underpromise and overdeliver. Be certain you also don't bite off more than you can chew. I'd recommend that you commit to half to three-quarters of what you believe you can do. Consider promising a certain number of projects or hours, then do them faster, better, and more thoroughly than what most would consider "standard."

Your goal will be to learn all you can. But you may land a paid position in the process. Or even a chance to partner with your mentor. It happens. If you follow my advice, you'll be an anomaly in a world with shrinking standards. You'll stand out from the crowd, and you'll be in high demand.

From Apprentice to Owner?

I was once in a meeting where a successful 60-year-old entrepreneur complained about his inability to find a successor. He has a profitable local company, and his children have no interest in taking over when he retires. If he retires with no successor it means he shuts it down, leaving about a million dollars in value on the table.

This guy would love to mentor a young person. He would teach them his valuable trade and probably sell (or give) them his company if it goes well. He says he has tried to find someone like that for years, but to no avail. I am pretty certain someone could make more money on a path with this guy than through most paths that lead through a college degree.

Baby boomers own a large percentage of the small businesses in America. Many of them are ready to retire, or will be in the next decade, but they don't have a successor and can't locate one. Many millennials and Gen Z-ers have work preferences that don't match the skills needed to run these firms. As a result, many of these businesses will wither or just shut down.

This means millions of dollars of value will be squandered, and hundreds of thousands of younger people won't learn the skills and have the opportunities left vacant by this situation. What a waste. Both for the entrepreneur and the millions of young people who could have assumed those roles and found a great path to success and wealth.

A local real estate investor in Roanoke, Virginia, has a similar plight. He has owned and managed more than 30 single-family homes over the past several decades. He is in his 70s and ready to retire. He will probably just sell the houses to investors or tenants, but it would have been great if he could have imparted his vast knowledge and insights to someone who could have taken over his company and properties. It would have been a win-win, but there was no one to step in.

Will you step into a role like this and create a win-win for yourself and a self-storage entrepreneur? As I mentioned, tens of thousands of self-storage facilities are mom-and-pop owned, and many could be available for acquisition. Many more are owned and operated by small to mid-sized firms. If you learn some of this business through training and study, then humbly present yourself to be mentored by one of these owners, you may position yourself to learn a lot and perhaps acquire their company (and others) over time.

I think the value-add strategy could be a great fit for pursuing this path. If you can find a self-storage facility that is under-managed and under-marketed, has land for expansion, and is owned by someone who wants to transition toward retirement, this could be your opportunity. At the time of this writing, I know of a few facilities that fit this description (but they will likely be unavailable by the time you read this because they're being pursued for acquisition now).

I need to offer one stern warning about this "apprentice to owner" sub-path. Please don't let a mom-and-pop owner's bad operational ways rub off on you. And don't let them convince you of what can't be done. Many of these smalltime owners stay smalltime because they don't think outside the box. They are limited by their experience, and you don't want that to define you.

If you tread this route, do it with humility toward the owner, but with an eye to what needs to be overhauled and improved. Do it with an eye toward a self-storage coach or mastermind that can teach you how to innovate and take that facility to the next level.

What Makes a Great Coach or Mentor?

Your situation is unique, and you'll have to sort out all of the particular issues in your decision. The traits of a paid coach may be somewhat different from those of a mentor, but I think there's enough commonality that I can let you sort out the distinctions.

- **Industry/niche specific**: There aren't many options in the self-storage arena, but it would serve you well to focus your search there if this is the path you plan to take.
- **Clarity**: If you have a mentor, be sure you both set clear expectations. If it is a paid coach, I would recommend you join a program where the roadmap is upfront. I would hate for you to spend tens of thousands of dollars for a program that just goes with the flow. It is best if the coach is systems-oriented. Caveat: You may get to a level someday where your coach just helps you with whatever you need at the time. Tom Brady, Michael Jordan, and Tiger Woods all come to mind. I'm guessing they had moved way beyond a set program with their coaches. (Think deeply about the fact that they all had coaches... though they were each the best in their fields.)
- **Results-focused**: Find a coach who will drive you toward a tangible goal. You need more than a cheerleader. This will be a coach who follows a well-defined process that has been created and refined over the course of coaching many students.

- **Know what you're getting**: You may sign up for coaching under a big-name guy or gal. But you may actually be coached by someone else, someone with far less experience or ability. It's okay to have a different coach, but you may be disappointed if you aren't told this in advance.
- **Guarantee**: You and your paid coach may end up like oil and water. The coach should therefore provide some type of out. My paid coach had a 90-day guarantee. We could ask for our money back in those first three months or if we walked out the door before the end of their first quarterly two-day live event.
- **Underwriting help**: A $10,000 error can result in a $120,000 loss in value (or worse) at today's cap rates. On the flip side, a lack of confidence could cause a student to back away from a great deal. A good coach or mentor can help.
- **Team**: When you get a deal under contract, you may have 90 days to close. That is not enough time to put together a good support team to close and start operating the deal. Some coaching programs have a team in place to help students with these issues if needed. When I closed my first deal after paid coaching, I leaned heavily on the team to help underwrite, perform due diligence, get a loan, raise equity, establish asset management, select property managers, and much more.
- **Assess your role in your success**: I know a guy who paid $100,000 for a mastermind program that guaranteed he would get his first deal. It's been years, and the deal has never come. Frustrated, he asked for and got a different coach within the mastermind. He is still disappointed. If you ask him, he would say the mastermind failed him. If you ask the mastermind leader, he may say that my friend has not done all the work to make it happen. He would perhaps point to a dozen or more other students who have done deals and are well on their way to abundant prosperity.
- **Practitioner and teacher**: Syndicated real estate, self-storage, and other commercial real estate opportunities have skyrocketed in popularity since the Great Recession. A rising tide lifts all boats. Paid coaches have come out of the woodwork as well. Some great teachers with limited experience have risen to prominence. They may not serve you well when things go poorly. Others are great practitioners, but they're not gifted teachers. Go for both.
- **Accountability**: Some self-storage students know they will go back to flipping single-family houses or stay with their W-2 job if they

don't have someone holding their feet to the fire. A great coach will have systems in place to hold students accountable.

- **Brutal honesty**: Sometimes you need the double-barreled truth. But it's possible that those who earn a living from their students may be reluctant to give it. The result could be that you go on in your blindness and don't reach your potential. I mean, how hard was it for Neil Peart's new coach to tell the greatest drummer of all time that he held his sticks wrong and should start over from scratch? How hard was it for the aging Rush drummer to accept that advice? Several years ago, I was living in a fantasy about how to raise capital for deals. I believed I could rely on a few mega-investors in Asia. My paid coach warned me repeatedly that I needed to develop a large cross section of investors, but I kept rebuffing him (and then I wondered why I was failing). One day, on a coaching call with two of my staff on the line, my coach said: "I've told you what to do for over two years. Don't call me again until you've done what I said!" That really stung. But it was exactly what I needed to hear. I finally took action, and it set me on a course for the success I'm experiencing today.

- **References**: As I mentioned earlier, check their references carefully. Don't just contact the references they gave you. Go online to see what everyone is saying about them. Don't let confirmation bias cloud your vision and cause you to only look for evidence to back your decision. Track down investors in the BiggerPockets community to see what others have experienced with this coach. They should have a system that has been proven with others along with testimonials to that effect.

- **Character, not just competence**: There are successful people that are well known for their wealth but not their integrity. Go for both. But definitely make sure they have stellar integrity.

- **Gut over hype**: In a prior decade, I asked someone I trusted for a reference on a great sales coach. He sent me to the best guy he knew. My initial read on the guy was not that positive, but I respected the source so much that I went down the road with him anyway. As the sales trainer pitched me, several warning bells went off. I didn't believe some things he promised, and his fee was steep. I ignored my gut and hired him anyway. It was a complete waste of time and money, setting me back in the eyes of my team. Don't ignore your gut feeling (or your spouse/partner).

Who Is an Ideal Candidate for Mentoring?

This path is certainly among my favorites. I have paid $25,000 for two different paid coaches in two different stages of my career. And I recently spent $25,000 to join a high-level real estate mastermind. Both of my coaching experiences led to profitable progress, and both pointed me to where I am today.

Last year, my business partner stayed in the home of a super-successful private equity fund manager on the slopes of a Colorado ski resort. The guy told him that he had been doing just fine on his own. Then he hired a strategy coach, and his business took off, skyrocketing his firm to another level. I recently spent $10,000 for the first year of the same program, and I have high hopes for growing in this arena for years to come.

If you have a steep learning curve in front of you, mentoring or paid coaching could be a great option. If you have the financial resources and the time to commit to a program like this, I recommend you consider it. If you are considering college and would look at an alternative path (coaching/mentoring), then this may be a route for you. Like I said, my son was mentored first, which confirmed his interest and aptitude, and then got a college degree in that field.

I heard about someone who went to four years of undergraduate school then three years of law school. He had apparently never set foot in a lawyer's office when he showed up for his first day of work. After only a month in his new career, he realized he hated it. And as he looked ahead at what his bosses and their bosses did, he believed he'd hate what they do too. He faced the painful reality that he'd just spent seven years and well over a $100,000 to train for a career he didn't want to do. He quit his job and tried to figure out his next steps. He recalled a brief stint in a teaching role, and he realized this made his soul come alive. Maybe this would be his path. He decided to go back to school to become a teacher.

I believe this young man's anguish could have been avoided if he would have inserted a season of coaching/mentoring into his equation early on. Perhaps an internship at a law firm during his undergraduate studies would have opened his eyes sooner. Unfortunately, I don't know how his story turned out.

Inna Rubinchik learned a similar lesson. But I do know how her story turned out, and it is one of my favorite real estate mentoring stories. I think you'll love it too.

Inna's Story: An Immigrant Who Found Success as an Entrepreneur

This is one of my favorite success stories in the realm of coaching and mentoring. It speaks to the power of mentoring as well as the determination it takes to go from meager beginnings to success through wise choices and hard work. If Inna Rubinchik can do what she's done in a little over a decade, then I believe you can do virtually anything you set your mind to.

Who is Inna Rubinchik? Inna is an immigrant from Russia. She came to America with just an overpacked suitcase at 14, but she was determined to do whatever it took to be successful. She's a real estate success story, but she didn't start out in real estate at all.

Inna originally got a master's in taxation and went to work for Deloitte in 2004. By 2008 she was a senior tax consultant. Inna led a team who uncovered a massive tax-saving opportunity for a prominent international client. They spent hundreds of hours over many days and nights researching and putting together the information needed to present this to the company's CFO. Inna and the team made their presentation then excitedly awaited his response. He basically shrugged his shoulders and went on to the next item of business. This felt like a punch in the gut to Inna and her team.

That's the day Inna knew she had to get out of corporate America. She wanted to take control of her destiny and was determined to do something that made a difference for her clients. She knew she wanted to work in real estate but had no idea how to get into the business. It didn't help that it was 2008, and the nation was plunging into a financial crisis.

Determined to figure out her future, Inna looked for work in San Francisco, California, for almost a year. She decided her future would be in commercial real estate, specifically in the arena of asset management. She ripped a handful of pages from the phone book (remember those?) and circled the real estate investment firms. She researched them all online then emailed 40 of them. She only received four replies, which resulted in three interviews. She walked into her last interview to meet seven partners of a prestigious San Francisco real estate investment firm. They offered her a 90-day unpaid internship with the possibility of a permanent position afterward. Inna's mentorship was on.

Inna started the next morning. She dove into her assignments. The firm managed a billion-dollar high-end office portfolio, and she learned as much about the business as possible. She learned how to underwrite properties for purchase, how to work with brokers, how to onboard new properties, and much more. Her goal was to work harder than the paid employees and to make herself indispensable to the firm.

Before long, the partners could see what a valuable employee she was. In the midst of her 90 unpaid days, they offered her $1,000 monthly. Soon it was increased to $2,000. At the completion of 90 days she was offered $6,500 per month to stay onboard. Inna was at the firm for the next five years.

Along the way, Inna became pregnant and was looking for more flexibility. The firm needed a manager for a 25-unit luxury property, and she landed the role. Over the next two years, Inna reached a new level in the arena of marketing, sales, tenant leasing, and ongoing management.

Inna realized she had the talent to do this for herself. In a burst of entrepreneurial energy, she set out on her own. Inna created the Leasing Agent 415 brand, and she sailed to the top of the local market in less than five years. She is the No. 1 leasing agent in the competitive San Francisco market. She leased the most highly priced residential condo in San Francisco history at $23,000 per month. She has over 200 deals to her name with a total rental value of over $25 million.

Inna was educated in accounting. She practiced in taxation. But she found her calling and destiny through boldly seeking out an unpaid mentorship. Now she is her own boss and is achieving the financial freedom many people only dream about. Though Inna started off at the bottom, she's made it to the top. She was willing to sacrifice in the short run to reach her long-term goals.

A final word...

The mentor path, perhaps more than others, may position you to take another of the paths simultaneously or later. For example, many students in the coaching program with me went on to find deals for other operators (Path 3). A few partnered with operators to raise capital for their deals (Path 4). Others took the slow road up the mountain (Path 1).

Is a mentor part of your success equation? Perhaps you'll start there, become a commercial real estate mogul, and end up coaching and mentoring others someday! Though that may not sound appealing right now, there may come a day when you want to leave a legacy and help others achieve the success you have enjoyed. Finishing this book may be the first step on your path.

CHAPTER 16

THE ROAD AHEAD

Are you ready to invest in a self-storage facility? Or buy one? Or start a chain? If so, you're in good company.

When I discuss self-storage with a variety of investors, operators, and some skeptics, I've heard several concerns about what the future of the industry holds. I think these concerns are valid:

- Will fully automated kiosk systems take the place of virtually all facility staff?
- Will automated self-storage management systems replace the current manual storage and retrieval methodology?
- Will storage and delivery-on-demand services eclipse the current model?

I'm not willing to go on record with a prediction here. But I will restate what you already know: *Change is coming.* That has always been and always will be true. Innovation and flexibility are necessary pillars of a successful business or investment strategy.

The fear of innovation is not a reason to sit on the sidelines. It is often the case that insiders—those who already have a strong market share— are best positioned to be innovators.

Consider this not only a warning but also encouragement. Being keenly aware of potential opportunities can help all of us stay agile and benefit from inevitable disruptions rather than ignoring them and losing out.

So far, I've made the case for self-storage as a powerful real estate investment vehicle. I've demonstrated how operators can successfully view their investment as an actively run quasi-retail business with numerous opportunities to add value and force appreciation. We've considered seven different paths you can follow to jump into the business yourself. Which is the best path for you?

Though there are many systems and tools that can help you on your path to success, you alone have the power to decide whether you are living your ultimate life. Are you living out your calling or just collecting a paycheck because someone else expects you to? Regardless of what you're doing now and where you go from here, I encourage you to reach out and take hold of your life. Don't be a bystander watching it unfold. You have been given talents and training and time. I hope that you capitalize on all of them to fulfill your destiny.

ABOUT THE AUTHOR

After graduating with an engineering degree from Marietta College and earning an MBA from The Ohio State University, Paul Moore entered the management development track at Ford Motor Company in Detroit, Michigan. From there he left to start a staffing company with a partner. Before selling it to a publicly traded firm five years later, Paul was a finalist for Ernst & Young's Michigan Entrepreneur of the Year two years in a row.

Paul later entered the real estate sector, where he flipped over 60 homes and 25 high-end waterfront lots; rehabbed and managed rental properties; built a number of new homes; developed a subdivision, and created two successful online real estate marketing firms. He also built a number of other companies and made quite a few medium- and high-risk investments along the way. Some paid off while others did not.

Lessons learned during the downturn guided him to the relative stability of the commercial real estate sector. Three successful commercial real estate projects led him into the arena of multifamily investing. The overheated market in multifamily later resulted in Paul's shift to self-storage and mobile home park investing. He launched and manages Wellings Capital, a firm that manages several funds that invest in these asset classes. Its income and growth funds have opened the door for passive investors to enjoy the unique safety, tax advantages, and profitability of these recession-resistant commercial investment classes.

Paul is a frequent guest on real estate and finance podcasts, a popular blogger for BiggerPockets (the web's leading real estate investment site), and a contributor to Fox Business. He also cohosted a wealth-building podcast called *How to Lose Money* for four years.

A portion of the profit from Paul's business is funneled into a number of world-changing causes. Their objectives include placing orphans in homes, ending human trafficking, and raising the standard of living for the impoverished around the world.

ACKNOWLEDGEMENTS

Just like running a business and investing in commercial real estate, writing a book is a team effort. I'm very grateful to my family—they have endured countless evenings and weekends of my distraction for "Dad's focus time."

I'm grateful to our team at Wellings Capital for your dreams and sacrifices that have made our business possible and our investors happy. Thanks, Ben Kahle, for believing in me and hanging with me through years of low pay and boring work. Your loyalty is paying off. I want to thank our operators who are doing the hard work of acquiring, financing, and running the properties in which we invest. Your efforts make our system work. And to our investors who believed in us before the evidence was in: We're so grateful for you, and we couldn't have walked this road without you!

Of course, this book would be not be what it is without the amazing stories from the real estate syndicators featured in these pages. I'm grateful to each one of you and your teams. I want to thank Kris Benson and Todd Allen, who were the first to introduce me to self-storage and patiently endured my many questions. I want to thank Matthew Ricciardella, who gave me insight into his remarkable work as a syndicator. I also want to thank Kris Bennett, who originally developed the chapter 2 analysis for 10 Federal. This was a real eye-opener for me and helped crystalize my thinking about multifamily versus self-storage.

I want to express my deep appreciation for BiggerPockets. My partnership with you over the last five years has provided a rich avenue of joy to me and an opportunity to interact with scores of real estate investors at every level. I want to specifically thank the publishing team, including Katie Miller, Kaylee Walterbach, and Savannah Wood, as well as Kim Ledgerwood, Wendy Dunning, Jarrod Jemison, Louise Collazo, Elizabeth Frels, and Katie Golownia. Of course, I want to thank other BiggerPockets team members including Nikki Frick and Jamie Wiebe. And, obviously, I owe a great debt to Josh Dorkin and Scott Trench for making all of this possible in the first place.

Most importantly, I want to thank my Creator for the opportunity to have this great life and to enjoy my work so much. I'll never be able to thank you enough!

More from
BiggerPockets Publishing

The Book on Negotiating Real Estate

When the real estate market gets hot, the investors who know the ins and outs of negotiating will get the deal. J Scott, Mark Ferguson, and Carol Scott combine real-world experience and the science of negotiation in order to cover all aspects of the negotiation process and maximize your chances of reaching a profitable deal.

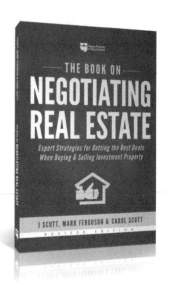

Real Estate Note Investing

Are you a wholesaler, a rehabber, a landlord, or even a turnkey investor? *Real Estate Note Investing* will help you turn your focus to the "other side" of real estate investing, allowing you to make money without tenants, toilets, and termites! Investing in notes is the easiest strategy to earn passive income. Learn the ins and outs of notes as investor Dave Van Horn shows you how to get started—and find huge success—in the powerful world of real estate notes!